H-8 Programming for Beginners

H-8 Programming for Beginners

Ron Santore, Don Inman and Bob Albrecht

dilithium Press
Portland, Oregon

© Copyright, dilithium Press, 1980

10 9 8 7 6 5 4 3 2 1

All rights reserved. No part of this book may be reproduced in any form or by any means without permission in writing from the publisher, with the following two exceptions: any material may be copied or transcribed for the non-profit use of the purchaser; and material (not to exceed 300 words and one figure) may be quoted in published reviews of this book.

ISBN: 0-918398-17-7
Library of Congress catalog card number: 80-68530

Printed in the United States of America.

dilithium Press
30 N.W. 23rd Place
Portland, Oregon 97210

QA76.8
.I53
S26

Preface

This book will teach you how to program the computer in its own built-in language. 'This language is called *machine language*, the most fundamental of all computer languages.' It consists of instructions expressed in binary, octal, or hexadecimal code.

You will learn how to write machine language programs for computer systems that use the INTEL 8080 microprocessor. One such system is the Heathkit H8 Computer. We assume you have an H8 computer with 4K of memory and you would like to learn how to use it. No terminal or mass storage of any kind is required for this course.

You can also use this book to learn how to program other 8080 based computers such as the ALTAIR 8800, IMSAI 8080, POLYMORPHIC 88, SOL 20 and many others. If you are using an 8080 based computer other than the Heathkit H8, consult the reference manual of your computer for differences in operation before entering your programs.

This book is broken up into four main sections:

Section 1: Introduction, terms, and first level programming;
Section 2: Subroutines, and level two programming;
Section 3: Level three programming, and games;
Section 4: Tables and references.

Throughout the book you will learn to write short machine language programs. You will test these programs by entering them into the Heathkit H8 computer by means of the front panel keyboard and viewing your results on the display lights.

If "machine language" sounds a little scary—don't worry, we're going to explain things as we go along; so just pay attention to details, take your time, and have fun....

The Heathkit H8 Computer.

We assume that you are using a minimum H8 system with the H8 panel monitor (PAM-8) in ROM, 4096 (4K) bytes of RAM, a front panel, a keyboard and a nine digit display as shown in the figure below.

The display is made up of 9 digits in three groups of three digits each. The keyboard contains 16 numerals and control keys. Both of these are described in section 3-1, page 14, along with instructions for using them.

Preface

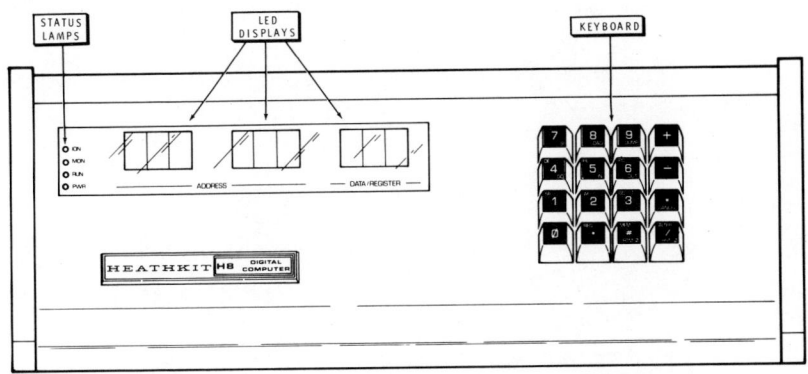

The H8 Front Panel.

Contents

Section One

1	Architecture, Bits and Bytes	1
2	Addressing	5
3	The PAM-8 Monitor	13
4	Registers (MVI A, STA, HLT, LDA, ADI)	25
5	Registers (MVI, MOV)	43
6	Registers (ADD, SUB, INR, DCR)	53

Section Two

7	Introduction	59
8	Flowcharts, Counters (JMP, SUI, NOP)	63
9	PAM-8 Subroutines (BEEP, DELAY, CALL, RETURN)	77
10	The Status Word and Flag Bits	85
11	Conditional Jumps (JZ, JNZ, JC, JNC, JP, JM)	95
12	Input Subroutine, Guessing Game	103
13	Random Number Generator, Output Subroutine	109

Section Three

14	Review	115
15	Register Pairs (LXI, INX, DCX, RRC, RLC)	117
16	AND/OR Logic (ANI, ORI)	123
17	More Random Numbers (XRA)	127
18	Dice	131
19	HI-LO, General Purpose Output Routine	137
20	Stars	141

Section Four

Appendix
  I The 8080 Op-Codes in Review   149
  II The Hexadecimal System   161
  III Sample Program   163
  IV A Better Random Number Generator   165
  V ASCII Codes   167
  VI Answers to Questions   169
  VII 8080 Reference Table   191
    Index   193

SECTION ONE

Chapter One

Architecture, Bits and Bytes

WHAT IS A COMPUTER?

All computers are made up of three main parts: the central processor, the terminal or display, and the memory.

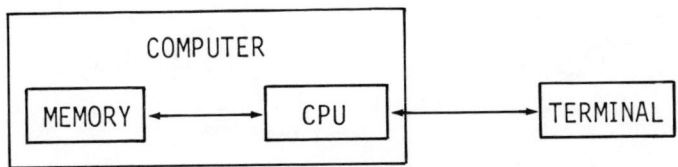

In your H8 computer the terminal/display is the front panel. With the front panel you can feed information into the computer using the touch-pad keys, and the computer can send information back to you using the LED displays.

The central processor is the 8080 integrated circuit, which is the heart of the whole computer. The central processor, sometimes called the CPU, contains eight *registers* which are temporary storage places for data. The eight registers are named B, C, D, E, H, L, FLAG word, and the ACCUMULATOR. In this text you will learn to instruct the central processor to move data around among the registers, the memory, and the terminal. That's programming.

BITS AND BYTES

Deep down inside, computers use a very simple code called "binary" to represent information. Binary is very simple: it uses only the two symbols 0 and 1 to represent all information. The symbols 0 and 1 are called binary digits, or "bits."

A bit is a binary digit.   A bit can only be 0 or 1.

A bit can be represented by a light. A light can only be on or off—throughout this book a light which is off will represent a binary 0, a light which is on will represent a binary 1.

Light off represents 0.   Light on represents 1.

A bit can also be represented by a switch. A switch can be either off or on. Again, we will use off to represent a binary 0, and on to represent a binary 1.

Switch off represents 0.   Switch on represents 1.

In a typical computer, information is stored in the memory of the computer. The memory is made up of memory locations or addresses.

Each memory location can store 8 bits of data.
A group of 8 bits is called a byte.
In other words, 8 bits = 1 byte.

A computer will usually store several thousand bytes of information, but remember that a byte is really composed of eight individual bits. A byte might look like: 0 1 1 0 0 0 1 1.

1 BYTE = 8 BITS

Since a bit can be represented by one light or one switch, a byte can be represented by *eight* lights or switches:

A byte is a pattern of ones and zeros. Here are some sample bytes:

01010011   10001111   01111111   11101110

Architecture, Bits and Bytes

Examine the above bytes for a minute. Do you think you could remember them? It's hard for humans to deal with all those ones and zeros—for one thing it's boring! But if you were a computer, binary would be your native language. Yes, computers love all those ones and zeros but people find them tedious and hard to remember. So...in the next section we'll tell you about a shorthand way to remember all those bits.

Chapter Two

Addressing

SPLIT OCTAL NOTATION

Octal shorthand is based on the number 8. It uses eight symbols called octal digits: 0, 1, 2, 3, 4, 5, 6 and 7 to represent binary numbers. Notice that in octal there is *no* symbol 8 or 9. Just as a binary digit must be only 0 or 1, an octal digit must be one of the numbers 0 to 7. Study this table:

DECIMAL #	OCTAL #	BINARY #
0	0	000
1	1	001
2	2	010
3	3	011
4	4	100
5	5	101
6	6	110
7	7	111

Please *memorize* the above table; you will use the binary numbers from zero to seven throughout your programming life.

An eight-bit binary number is written in octal notation by breaking it up into three sections. The following are those hard-to-remember bytes from page two:

01010011	becomes	01 010 011
10001111	becomes	10 001 111
01111111	becomes	01 111 111
11101110	becomes	11 101 110

Very well (you say...), but why? You'll soon find that it's much easier to remember the octal digits than the binary ones.

Now let's write the octal sections from above into octal numbers:

BINARY #	3 PIECES	OCTAL #
01010011	01 010 011	123
10001111	10 001 111	217
01111111	01 111 111	177
11101110	11 101 110	356

Is 123 easier to remember than 01010011?

EXERCISE

Fill in the blanks on the following:

```
11010001 = 11 010 001 = 321
10000100 = 10 000 100 = 204
00100001 = _____ = ___
11010011 = _____ = ___
00111000 = _____ = ___
11000111 = _____ = ___
```

Addressing

```
303 = 11 000 011 = 11000011
377 = 11 111 111 = 11111111
042 = _____ = _____
311 = _____ = _____
257 = _____ = _____
176 = _____ = _____
```

If you have been following closely, you now know how to interpret a byte as a binary number, a decimal number, or an octal number. Throughout the book we will use octal notation as a shorthand for binary. In places where confusion might occur we will use "B" to indicate Binary and "Q" for Octal. For instance, 101B is a binary number and 101Q is octal.

ADDRESSING MEMORY

Computer memory can be though of as a bank of empty storage boxes. Each box has a location or address, and each box will hold one data byte.

In the H8, memory locations are identified by a 16 bit number. So to specify an address in memory, *two bytes* must be used. Suppose you want to represent the 16 bit binary address

0110110010100111B as a split octal number. The binary number is first split into two bytes:

16 bit binary: 0110110010100111
two bytes: 01101100 10100111

Then each byte is converted to octal, as previously shown on page 5.

binary: 01 101 100, 10 100 111
octal: 2 5 4, 2 4 7

Here's another example:

16 bit binary: 0010000001000000
two bytes: 00100000 01000000
binary: 00 100 000, 01 000 000
octal: 0 4 0, 1 0 0

Pay special attention to the above; the beginner sometimes wants to convert the 16 bit address directly to octal—and that's wrong. The 16 bit number *must* first be split into two bytes, and then each byte is converted to octal. This method (split octal) is used in most modern 8 bit computers.

To find the binary equivalent of a split octal number, first change each 3 digit octal number to its binary equivalent, and then combine the binary parts to form the 16 bit address. For example:

octal: 0 4 0, 1 0 0
binary: 00 100 000, 01 000 000
combined: 00100000 01000000

EXERCISE

Convert each 16 bit binary number to split octal. Just follow the procedure you learned above.

16 bit binary: 1110110011010001
two bytes: __ ___ ___   __ ___ ___
octal: _____   _____

Addressing

```
16 bit binary: 0011111001010011
   two bytes: __ ___ ___   __ ___ ___
        octal: _____    _____

16 bit binary: 1111100011111111
   two bytes: __ ___ ___   __ ___ ___
        octal: _____    _____
```

In split octal, three octal digits are used to represent eight bits, or one byte. To represent 16 bits (two bytes) two distinct sets of three octal digits each are used; in other words, it takes three octal digits to equal a byte, and it takes six octal digits to equal one address.

In the exercise below, convert each split octal address to the equivalent address in binary:

```
040 100 = __ ___ ___   __ ___ ___ = _____   _____
077 377 = __ ___ ___   __ ___ ___ = _____   _____
041 245 = __ ___ ___   __ ___ ___ = _____   _____
036 260 = __ ___ ___   __ ___ ___ = _____   _____
```

Another way to view the split octal number notation is through the counting process. This may make things a little clearer:

```
SPLIT OCTAL        BINARY
  000 000     = 00000000 00000000
  000 001     = 00000000 00000001
  000 002     = 00000000 00000010
  000 003     = 00000000 00000011
       •              •
       •              •
       •              •
  000 377     = 00000000 11111111
```

Now we've filled one byte completely with 1's and the right half of the split octal number is 377. When we add one more, we get:

```
  001 000     = 00000001 00000000
```

Here's a summary table:

SPLIT OCTAL	BINARY
000 000	= 00000000 00000000
000 001	= 00000000 00000001
.	.
.	.
.	.
000 377	= 00000000 11111111
001 000	= 00000001 00000000
001 001	= 00000001 00000001
.	.
.	.
.	.
001 377	= 00000001 11111111
002 000	= 00000010 00000000
002 001	= 00000010 00000001
.	.
.	.
.	.
377 376	= 11111111 11111110
377 377	= 11111111 11111111

With sixteen bits to work with, 377 377 is the largest octal number that can be written. It is important to realize that in *split* octal, the sixteen bit number is first split into two groups and then converted to octal. The largest number each byte can be is 377Q. In split octal, the number 400Q (and anything larger) is not allowed.

There is another shorthand system commonly used to represent 8 bit bytes — it's called Hexadecimal. If you're interested in how the Hexadecimal system relates to Octal refer to Appendix II. In this course we will use the octal shorthand system.

SELF TEST

1. In this book we will frequently represent one byte, or eight bits, by an octal code consisting of ____ (how many) octal digits?

Addressing

2. Suppose $Q_2Q_1Q_0$ is a three digit octal code representing one byte or eight bits. What are the possible values for each digit? We have done the first one for you.
   a. Q_0? 0, 1, 2, 3, 4, 5, 6, 7
   b. Q_1? _____
   c. Q_2? _____

3. Write the octal equivalent for each eight-bit binary number.
   a. 00000001B = _____ Q
   b. 00001000B = _____ Q
   c. 01000000B = _____ Q
   d. 01001001B = _____ Q
   e. 10011100B = _____ Q
   f. 01111111B = _____ Q

4. If possible, write the eight-bit binary number (byte) that is equivalent to each octal number. However, if the octal number *cannot* be expressed as a byte (8 bits), write, "not possible."
   a. 007Q = _____ B
   b. 123Q = _____ B
   c. 411Q = _____ B
   d. 377Q = _____ B
   e. 600Q = _____ B

5. Write each 16 bit binary number as a six digit *split-octal* number.
   a. 0000000100000000B = _____ Q
   b. 0000000011100101B = _____ Q
   c. 0101001111010001B = _____ Q
   d. 1111111100000000B = _____ Q

6. Write each split octal number as a 16 bit binary number:
   a. 111 222Q = _____ B
   b. 040 106Q = _____ B
   c. 076 123Q = _____ B
   d. 262 300Q = _____ B

7. Some of the following are valid split octal numbers, others are not possible. For each one write "OK" or "NO."
   a. 377 377Q _____
   b. 077 077Q _____
   c. 123 321Q _____
   d. 244 444Q _____
   e. 077 777Q _____
   f. 045 306Q _____
   g. 543 000Q _____

8. Complete the following counting table:
   047 373Q   00100111 11111011B
   047 374Q   00100111 11111100B
   047 375Q   _____ _____
   ___ ___   _____ _____
   ___ ___   _____ _____
   ___ ___   _____ _____
   ___ ___   _____ _____

9. What is the largest number that can be written using eight bits in binary: _____; in octal: _____.

Chapter Three

The PAM-8 Monitor

The front panel on your H8 computer is made up of two parts, the keyboard and the display. The front panel monitor (PAM-8) is a *program* stored in the computer in permanent memory (ROM memory). A monitor is a machine language program that allows you to examine and modify memory or any of the eight CPU registers. In other words, the PAM-8 front panel monitor is a program which will aid us in writing our other programs.

Below is a reproduction of your display panel. Look at the display and the labels under it. The display is made up of nine digits, organized as three groups of three digits each. Each group displays the octal equivalent of one byte (eight bits). The octal information displayed may be the *contents* of a memory location or of a register, or it may be the *address* of a memory location. The PAM-8 program converts all binary numbers to their octal equivalent for display on the front panel.

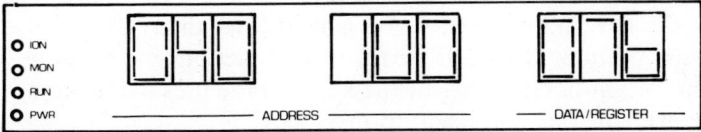

Each data byte is displayed as an octal number in the range 000Q to 377Q, equivalent to the binary numbers 0000000 to 11111111.

The H8 keypad has 16 keys arranged as shown in *ROM*. The keypad allows you to control the PAM-8 monitor. Some of its characteristics are:
- Each keystroke (one tap on a key) is acknowledged by a short "click."
- Certain keystrokes, or combinations of keystrokes, are acknowledged by a "beep."
- Holding a key down continuously repeats the key's function. (You will get a feel for the tap needed to avoid repetitions.)
- Octal digits are entered using the keys 0 through 7.
- The + key increments the memory or register by 1.
- The − key decrements the memory or register by 1.
- The * key cancels the previous keypad entry, to allow you to correct mistakes in pressing the keys.
- The ALTER key causes PAM-8 to enter the alter mode.
- The MEM key causes PAM-8 to enter the display memory mode.
- The REG key causes the PAM-8 to enter the register mode.

Some of the keys have several functions, depending on the PAM-8 mode being used. In the register mode, some numeric keys call the two registers shown in the upper left-hand corner of the key. When the PAM-8 is in neither the register nor the memory mode, the keys perform the functions indicated in the lower right-hand corner of the key. All the uses of the keys will be explained as you begin to use them.

The PAM-8 Monitor

You are now well enough informed to begin practicing with your H8. Turn the power on using the switch located on the back panel of the H8 computer. The steps that follow will tell you how to use the keypad on the front panel to store a data byte into a particular memory location.

Example: Store 111Q into memory location 040 100Q. (Remember that "Q" means octal.)

DO THIS	DISPLAY WILL SHOW	COMMENTS
1. Press #	XXX XXX XXX Note: "X" is used to mean that any digit may appear in that place.	You only need to "tap" the key. A decimal point will appear after each digit in the display. If you hold the key down too long, these points will come and go. In order to accept a memory address these points must be showing.
2. Press 0 4 0 1 0 0	040 100 XXX	You only need to tap the key; if you hold it down, PAM-8 will assume you want the same number repeated. The memory address you have just entered will appear in the two 3-digit displays to the left. Any number may appear where an "X" is shown.
3. Press /	040 100 XXX	Again, only a tap on the key is needed. Now the decimal point will appear to be running from right to left. This is your clue that PAM-8 is ready to accept a new entry for memory location 040 100Q. If you hold the ALTER key down too long, the moving decimal point will appear and disappear.
4. Press 1 1 1	040 101 XXX	Almost as soon as you finish tapping the "1" key three times for "111," the display will change to show the next higher memory location.

Congratulations! You have stored the number 111Q into memory location 040 100Q. Is it really stored there? You can find out by *examining* memory location 040 100Q.

Example: Examine memory location 040 100Q to see what data byte is stored there.

DO THIS	DISPLAY WILL SHOW	COMMENTS
1. Press #	040 101 XXX	A decimal point will appear after each digit in the display.
2. Press 0 4 0 1 0 0	040 100 111	You will find the "111" (entered there in the previous example) is indeed stored at location 040 100.

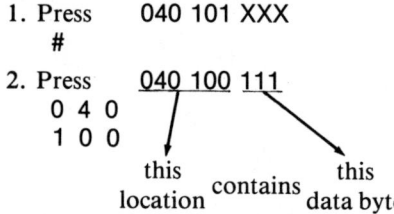

Exercise: Store the number 222Q into memory location 040 200Q. Where we have left blanks below copy the contents of the correct display into that space.

DO THIS	DISPLAY READS	COMMENTS
1. Press #	XXX XXX XXX	If the H8 has been turned off, there is no telling what will show up in memory or on the display. Otherwise, the last memory location and the data stored there will appear on the display. (And, of course, there will be a decimal point after each digit in the display.)
2. Press 0 4 0 2 0 0	___ ___ XXX	The memory location or address that you just entered would appear on the display. The decimal points disappear.
3. Press /	___ ___ XXX	The running decimal point should appear, which means that PAM-8 is ready for you to alter the contents or byte stored at the location entered in step two.
4. Press 2 2 2	___ ___ XXX	The decimal point keeps running, and the next higher memory address appears on the display, along with whatever happens to be stored at that location.

The PAM-8 Monitor

Exercise: Examine location 040 200Q and show the contents of the display in the blanks below.

1. Press #	040 200 XXX	The decimal points appear after each digit.
2. Press 0 4 0 2 0 0	___ ___ ___	Did the number you entered at this memory location appear in the right-most section of the display?

Discussion: You have seen that immediately after you enter a number at a particular memory address, the next higher memory address and the data byte stored there will appear on the display. This feature makes it a lot easier for you to enter numbers in successive memory locations without having to enter each and every memory address by hand. The usefulness of this feature will become more evident in the next chapter, when you will begin entering longer programs.

Example: The steps below will show you how to examine a memory location where you've just entered a number, without having to enter the address of that memory location another time.

DO THIS	DISPLAY READS	COMMENTS
1. Press #	040 200 222	The last address you examined and its contents should still show on the display. If not, repeat the last exercise so that the display reads as shown. The decimal points should appear after each digit.
2. Press 0 4 0 2 0 1	040 201 XXX	The memory location just entered will appear, the decimal points will disappear, and the byte that is stored at 040 201Q will be displayed in the three right-most digits.
3. Press /	040 201 XXX	The running decimal point appears, and the computer waits for you to alter the number at location 040 201Q.
4. Press 1 2 3	040 202 XXX	The next higher address and contents are displayed.

5. Press −	040 201 123	The minus key (−) decrements the memory address by one, and allows you to check the data you just entered.
6. Press −	040 200 222	Another tap on the minus key decrements the address again and allows you to view the previous memory location and data byte stored there.
7. Press +	040 201 123	You are now back to the memory location you entered in step 3. Notice the data byte is the same as the one you stored there in step 4.

Discussion: This is a simple way to move backward or forward among the memory locations to see what is stored in each one. If you need to move backward or forward several locations, hold the + or − key down until the address you are looking for appears, then release the key. Try this technique out before going any further.

MEMORY MAP

The computer's memory is made up of ROM (permanent memory) and RAM (scratch-pad memory). The ROM contains the PAM-8 monitor program, and the RAM is used by you, the programmer, to store your program.

A map of memory locations is shown below. It is important to notice that your programs are stored beginning at address 040 100Q.

The memory map shows you which locations are used by the PAM-8 front panel monitor. This program is located in ROM in memory locations 000 000Q to 004 000Q. (Remember, *Read Only Memory* contains programs and data that are always there and cannot be erased or changed.) From the memory map you can also see that locations 004 000Q to 040 000Q are reserved for future expansion, and an additional section from 040 000Q to 040 100Q is reserved for use by the PAM-8. The PAM-8 uses this last section as a scratch-pad for temporary storage of information. You the user, may use the RAM starting at memory location 040 100Q.

The PAM-8 Monitor 19

The H8 Computer

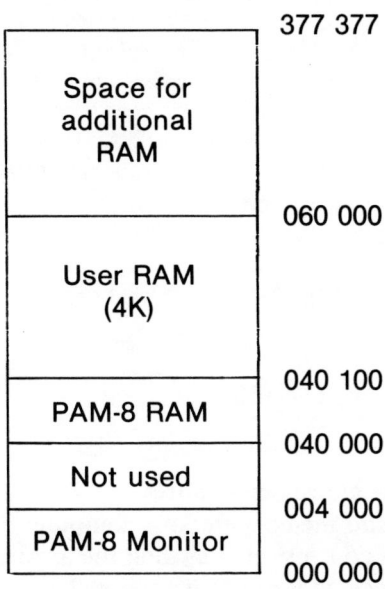

The memory map shows the upper limit of RAM as 060 000Q. Actually the last RAM memory address would be one byte lower, or 057 377Q. This is true if you have an H8 computer with 4K of RAM memory. There is an easy way to find the upper limit of RAM. A special register called the "stack pointer" (SP) is automatically set to the upper limit of RAM memory when power is first turned on. A complete discussion of the stack pointer will be covered later, but for now, we'll show you how to use the stack pointer to determine your highest RAM memory address.

Example: Find the upper memory limit in your H8.

1. Press •   XXX XXX SP   This puts the PAM-8 in register mode.

2. Press 1   XXX XXX SP   This key selects the register called the Stack Pointer, and tells you the memory location it is pointing to. When the H8 is turned on, the stack pointer will be pointing to the upper limit in the H8 memory. In the rightmost display, you will

see the letters SP which stand for Stack Pointer, and the memory address to which it is pointing will appear in the usual place on the display.

Exercise: Store the data byte 222Q into the non-existent memory location 377 377Q, then examine that location. What did you find there? Examine locations shown below and indicate their contents:

ADDRESS	CONTENT
377 377	_____
377 200	_____
377 150	_____
377 102	_____

All four of the above octal addresses are invalid memory addresses; there is no memory in your computer at that address. Can you draw a conclusion regarding the apparent contents of an invalid memory address? Is it random?

In the next section of the book, you will be storing instructions and data in consecutive memory locations. The following example will give you practice in using the front panel to store, examine, and correct a series of entries in consecutive memory locations.

Example: Store the data bytes 000Q, 111Q through 777Q in consecutive memory locations starting at address 040 100Q and ending at address 040 107Q.

1. Press #   XXX XXX XXX   Enter the MEM mode.

2. Press   040 100 XXX   Examine address 040 100Q.
   0 4 0
   1 0 0

3. Press /   040 100 XXX   Decimal point is running.

4. Enter   040 101 XXX   As soon as you enter your data
   0 0 0   byte (000Q), the address
                                      increments.

5. Enter   040 102 XXX
   1 1 1

The PAM-8 Monitor

6. Enter   040 103 XXX
   2 2 2

and so on to 777Q.

Discussion: You have stored the octal numbers 000Q, 111Q, 222Q, 333Q, 444Q, 555Q, 666Q, and 777Q into memory locations 040 100Q through 040 107Q. Did you make any mistakes when entering those numbers? Find out by examining addresses 040 100Q through 040 107Q. Check the display at each step and record the observed values in the blanks provided below... don't make any corrections at this time.

1. Press   XXX XXX XXX
    #
2. Press   040 100 <u>000</u>
   0 4 0
   1 0 0
3. Press   040 101 _____
    +
4. Press   040 102 _____
    +
5. Press   040 103 _____
    +
6. Press   040 104 _____
    +
7. Press   040 105 _____
    +
8. Press   040 106 _____
    +
9. Press   040 107 _____
    +

Discussion: You will notice that starting at address 040 104Q the numbers observed are not the same as the ones that were entered. What happened? Well, remember that you are entering the octal equivalent of eight bit binary numbers. Since the lead group of an eight bit binary number expressed in octal holds only *two* bits, the computer only interprets the last two bits of the leading number you enter in octal. For example, 444Q is 100100100B. However, the computer only looks at eight bits and sees 00100100B. The leading bit has been lost at the time of entering 444Q—in other words, although you entered 444Q on the keypad, you actually entered 044Q into the computer's memory. The same thing happened when you entered 555Q, 666Q, and 777Q. The *ninth* (leftmost) bit was omitted. Refer to page 10 and remember that the largest octal byte that is valid is 377Q.

Example: Follow the steps below to enter numbers in consecutive memory locations:

1. Press   #
2. Enter 040 200
3. Press   /
4. Enter 004
5. Enter 005
6. Enter 006
7. Enter 007
8. Enter 010
9. Enter 020

Now examine locations 040 200Q through 040 205Q to see that your entries were correct. Let's say that in memory location 040 203Q we meant to enter 010Q (not 007Q) and in 040 204Q we meant to enter 020Q (not 010Q) and in 040 205Q we meant to enter 030Q (not 020Q). How can you correct the entries? Follow the steps below:

1. Press   #
2. Enter 040 203
3. Press   /
4. Enter 010
5. Enter 020
6. Enter 030

Now, go back and examine the addresses 040 200Q through 040 205Q. Have the *corrections* been made in the correct memory locations?

You now know how to store data bytes into the H8. Since a machine language program is simply a list of particular bytes, you also know the procedure for storing a program into the H8.

In the next section you'll begin actual programming. Programming is simply writing the program, storing the instruction bytes in memory, examining the memory for errors, and correcting those errors. When the program is correctly stored in the

The PAM-8 Monitor

H8 memory, you'll tell the computer to execute or *run* the program.

SELF TEST

1. What key do you use before examining the contents of a memory location or before entering a memory location whose contents you wish to change?

2. What key do you use to prepare the computer to accept a number for the memory location that is now showing in the display?

3. What does a decimal point following every digit in the display tell you?

4. What does a running decimal point in the display indicate?

5. Suppose you follow the sequence of instructions given below. Fill in the blanks with the numbers which will appear in the display after performing the operation in that step.
   a. Press #   XXX XXX XXX
   b. Enter 040 234   ___ ___ XXX
   c. Press /   ___ ___ XXX
   d. Enter 333   ___ ___ XXX
   e. Press −   ___ ___ ___

6. You have entered the following numbers at the memory addresses shown:
   043 100   115
   043 101   116
   043 102   117
   043 103   120
   List the steps to address 043 102 and change the numbers stored at both 043 102 and 043 103 to 200 and 201 respectively.

Chapter Four

Registers (MVI A, STA, HLT, LDA, ADI)

LET'S GO

This chapter will introduce the use of the accumulator and memory with short, simple programs. The program itself is usually stored in memory in sequential order. Any area of available memory (RAM memory) may be chosen for the first instruction. The Heathkit H8 has memory available for the user starting at location 040 100Q as shown by the memory map on page 19. The figure below shows how the program is normally stored in sequential order in memory:

	ADDRESS	INSTRUCTION/DATA	
	040 100	XXX	
	040 101	XXX	
	040 102	XXX	
Address	040 103	XXX	The instructions
locations	040 104	XXX	and data used
given in	040 105	XXX	in the program
split-	040 106	XXX	will be placed in
octal			this area. Each
notation.	.	.	location holds
	.	.	*one* byte.
	.	.	

Regardless of what starting point is chosen, the program steps are placed in order from that point. For our purposes, we will use 040 100Q as the starting point for most programs. For the short introductory programs in this chapter we will need only a few memory locations.

Information can be stored in memory, but it can also be stored in temporary storage locations called *registers*. Registers are similar to memory locations but they are used for special purposes. They do not have an address, but are referred to directly by letters of the alphabet. The *Accumulator* is one example of a register, and it is by far the most useful one. The Accumulator is called register *A*, and it holds eight bits of information just as a memory address does. one of the purposes of the accumulator is that of a temporary storage place. Information is moved into the accumulator from various places — with your programming you could move a byte into the accumulator directly from the program, or directly from one of the other registers, or from a terminal, or from memory, or indirectly from memory by using two registers to indicate a memory location. While the byte is in the accumulator it may be modified in several ways. The program might add to it, subtract from it, shift the bits right or left, or change it in other ways. In our first example programs, we will not modify the data. We are only interested in transferring it to a certain memory address with no changes.

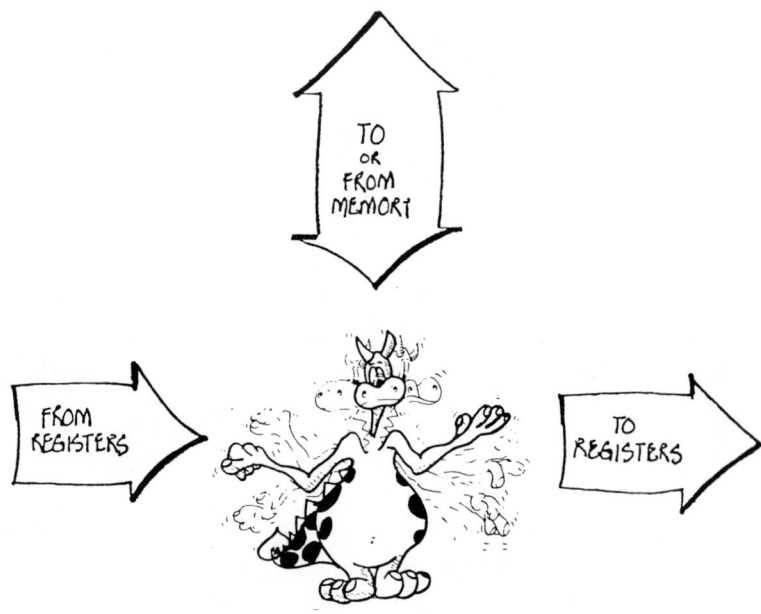

The Accumulator.

Registers

DEVELOPING A TYPICAL PROGRAM

The programming instructions you will be using are called *mnemonic op-codes*. Mnemonic codes are easy-to-remember alphabetic abbreviations for machine language instructions. You should memorize these abbreviations and the instructions they stand for as you go along. Most machine language programs are developed in steps:
1. Define what you want the program to do.
2. Write the program in mnemonic code.
3. Write the program in binary or octal.

For example:

Step 1: Let's write a program which will place a data byte into the accumulator, then move (or copy) that data byte to a location in memory, then stop.

Step 2: The *Move Immediate* instruction (MVI) will move one data byte into the accumulator. The MVI instruction is composed of two bytes — one for the instruction, and then a second byte for the data which is to be put into the accumulator.

The *Store Accumulator* instruction (STA) will store the contents of the accumulator into a memory address. STA requires three bytes — one for the instruction, and two more to specify the 16 bit address where the accumulator data is to be stored.

The *Halt* instruction (HLT) stops the computer.

For this example, let's move the data byte 01001001B (111Q) into the accumulator, and then transfer it to memory address 00100000 10000000B (040 200Q).

The program mnemonic op-codes look like:

```
MVI A,111
STA 040 200
HLT
```

Remember that the computer does not understand mnemonic instructions — only binary numbers. Therefore, the last step in writing a program is to translate the mnemonics into numbers that the computer can understand:

```
MVI A = 00111110B = 076Q
STA = 00110010B = 062Q
HLT = 01110110B = 166Q
```

You will find a table on page 195 containing all the op-codes used in this book and their octal equivalents. Pay special attention to the op-codes as they are introduced one-by-one in the book, and you won't have to refer to the table very much. 8080 op-codes are really very easy to remember; if you do all the exercises as we go along, you won't have any trouble remembering the most common codes.

Step 3: Translating the op-code mnemonics from Step 2, we get:

MNEMONIC	=	OCTAL	= BINARY	
MVI A,111		076	00111110	
		111	01001001	2 bytes
STA 040 200		062	00110010	
	notice →	200	10000000	3 bytes
		040	00100000	
HLT		166	01110110	1 byte

The program, as you will enter it, is shown in the column marked OCTAL. The PAM-8 monitor will convert the octal instructions into binary for you and will enter the instructions into the H8 computer's memory in binary. You can begin to appreciate the power and convenience of the PAM-8 by looking at the two columns above marked OCTAL and BINARY. Notice how many fewer digits there are in the column marked OCTAL! You will be entering those digits into the computer—they are the program.

Notice that the store memory address, 040 200Q, is stored in memory low order byte first. This is required by the 8080 CPU and all memory addresses must be stored this way if the program is to work properly.

Well, that completes the program...will it work? There's only one way to find out—try it.

Here are the steps to follow:

1. Decide where the program will be located.
2. Enter the program into memory.
3. Examine memory to check for correct entry.
4. Run the program.
5. Examine the results.

Registers

Step 1: Let's use the first address location recommended for H8 users—starting at 040 100Q. The programming instructions are placed in sequential order starting at 040 100Q as follows:

ADDRESS	OP-CODE	INSTRUCTION
040 100	076	MVI A,111
040 101	111	
040 102	062	STA 040 200
040 103	200	
040 104	040	
040 105	166	HLT

Step 2: Entering the program.
  a. Turn on the computer.
  b. Access memory location 040 100Q by pressing in order:
      #   0 4 0   1 0 0
  c. Key in order:
      /   0 7 6
            1 1 1
            0 6 2
            2 0 0
            0 4 0
            1 6 6   /

Step 3: Examine the program for correctness.
  a. Access the starting address again by pressing:
      #   0 4 0   1 0 0
  b. Check the value of the contents in the right three digits of the display:
  c. Press + key to access successive memory locations. Address is shown in the left six digits, contents in the right three digits.
  d. If any of the contents are incorrect, change them using the procedure on page 22.

Step 4: Run the program.
  a. Press in order:
      •   6   This accesses the Program Counter.
  b. Key in order:
      /   0 4 0   1 0 0   /   This sets the Program Counter to the starting address.
  c. Press:
      4   *GO* means execute or run the program.

Step 5: Next, get the answer or result. For this program, check the results in location 040 200 by pressing in order: # 0 4 0 2 0 0 . The right most three digits of the display should show 111Q. If the display is correct, then you entered and ran the program correctly — 111Q was moved from the accumulator to 040 200Q.

Let's see what the computer is doing by *tracing* its steps. We will make a chart of the storage compartments (registers) within the computer and fill them according to the instructions. Compartments will be needed for the accumulator and for memory address 040 200Q. We want to show what happens at each instruction: MVI, STA, HLT. When the contents of the accumulator or memory change we will show it in bold face type.

INSTRUCTION	ACCUMULATOR	MEMORY 040 200
040 100 MVI A 040 101 111	**111**	XXX
040 102 STA 040 103 200 040 104 040	111	**111**
040 105 HLT	111	111

BREAKPOINTS

In the first program we used the HLT instruction to stop the computer, in order to examine the results in memory. In longer programs, it's often useful to place HLT instructions at various places throughout the program in order to examine results or registers along the way. HLT's used in that manner are called *breakpoints*. Since the computer operates so fast, breakpoints are a good way to examine a program in steps, allowing you to follow the program as it runs.

Let's now insert a HLT after each instruction in the original program:

The New Program:

ADDRESS	OP-CODE	INSTRUCTION	
040 100	076	MVI A,111	
040 101	111		
040 102	166	HLT	New instruction.

Registers

```
040 103        062        STA 040 200
040 104        200
040 105        040
040 106        166        HLT
```

Enter the program into the computer and run it as we did on page 29. When the 4 key is pressed the computer will stop after the first instruction. At this time access the accumulator by keying: • 2 . The display should look like this:

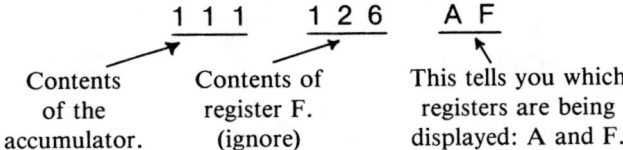

1 1 1	1 2 6	A F
Contents of the accumulator.	Contents of register F. (ignore)	This tells you which registers are being displayed: A and F.

Press • 6 and you will see that the contents of the program counter (PC in the display) are 040 103Q. This tells you that the computer is ready to execute the next instruction, which begins at memory address 040 103Q.

Now press 4 , and the computer will continue executing the program from the breakpoint. It will stop again at the next HLT, which is at the end of the program. Examine both the accumulator and location 040 200Q. What are their values?

Accumulator: ____ ____ ____
Address 040 200: ____ ____ ____

Notice that when the contents of the accumulator are moved to a memory location, the contents of the accumulator remains the same. The computer simply *copied* the contents of the accumulator into memory location 040 200Q.

EXPANDING THE PROGRAM

We will introduce one more instruction in this section. The accumulator can be loaded directly from a memory address. The *Load Accumulator* instruction (LDA) does this. The data at the specified memory location is loaded (or copied) into the accumulator. The data at the specified memory location does not change. To use this instruction, the data to be used should be placed in the specified memory location before it is loaded into A.

Let's add the LDA instruction to our original program. We will step through the program manually with a *trace* and then step through the program on the computer with the single-step function key.

Here is a summary of the instructions introduced so far, and an explanation of each:

MVI A	076 XXX	Move immediate to the accumulator.
STA	062 nnn mmm	Store the accumulator at address mmm nnn.
LDA	072 nnn mmm	Load the accumulator from address mmm nnn.
HLT	166	Halt operation.

Revised Program

ADDRESS	OP-CODE	INSTRUCTION
040 100	076	MVI A,111
040 101	111	
040 102	062	STA 040 200
040 103	200	
040 104	040	
040 105	076	MVI A,222
040 106	222	
040 107	062	STA 040 201
040 110	201	
040 111	040	
040 112	072	LDA 040 200
040 113	200	
040 114	040	
040 115	062	STA 040 202
040 116	202	
040 117	040	
040 120	062	STA 040 203
040 121	203	
040 122	040	

Registers

040 123	076	MVI A,333
040 124	333	
040 125	166	HLT

Now imagine that you are the computer. Go through the instructions in the program one-by-one and fill in the values in the trace chart below to show what happened after each instruction was executed. Answers are on page 172.

Trace Chart

Address	Contents of Accumulator	Contents of Memory Location			
		040 200	040 201	040 202	040 203
040 100					
040 102					
040 105					
040 107					
040 112					
040 115					
040 120					
040 123					
040 125					

Now, load the program into the computer. Next set the program counter to 040 100Q by pressing:

```
    •   6
    /   0 4 0   1 0 0   /
```

Then instead of pressing 4 to start the program, press the 7 key. The computer will execute the first instruction and then the program counter will go to the second instruction, which is at 040 102Q. (Remember, the first instruction consists of two bytes.)

The program counter started here:

⟶ 040 100   076
   040 101   111
   040 102   062
   040 103   200

Now it's moved to here:

```
    040 100   076
    040 101   111
 →  040 102   062
    040 103   200
    040 104   040
```

The program counter is a 16 bit register which is used to *point to* the next instruction to be executed. It is normally automatically incremented after each instruction in order to point to the next instruction. You will find out later that the programmer can alter the sequential operation of a program by changing the program counter. But for now, just remember that the program counter keeps track of the next instruction to be executed.

Even though the program counter moved to the second instruction at 040 102Q, the program only executed the first instruction at 040 100. Examine the contents of the accumulator. It should be 111Q since the first instruction is MVI A,111. This should also agree with your answer in the trace on page 33. That's the purpose of the trace—to make sure that the computer is doing exactly what you want it to, step by step.

Press the 7 key again and the program counter will go to 040 105Q. (The second instruction occupies three bytes.) The computer has just executed the STA 040 200 instruction. Check memory location 040 200Q and compare it with the value in your trace chart. They should be the same. The accumulator's contents (111Q) have been stored into memory address 040 200Q. Continue pressing the 7 key and checking the results with your trace.

You now have two different methods to check the proper execution of a program:
1. The breakpoint method—inserting HLT's.
2. The single step method—using the 7 key.

We have introduced two types of instructions so far, Direct (such as LDA and STA) and Immediate (such as MVI). There is a distinct difference between the two.

DIRECT INSTRUCTIONS

Often the data that is being used in a program is to be stored somewhere in memory or loaded from memory. You might

Registers

think of a direct instruction as giving directions as to where to store or find data. A second way to think of a direct instruction is that it gives the exact or *direct* memory location which is to be used. All instructions of this type are made up of three bytes. The first byte is the op-code which tells what's to be done (store, load, jump, and so on), and the second and third bytes give the direct address associated with the instruction. So far, we have used the STA (Store Accumulator Direct) and LDA (Load Accumulator Direct) instructions.

IMMEDIATE INSTRUCTIONS

There are times when we will know what data is to be used in advance of running a program. The use of a constant in an equation is an example of knowing in advance what a particular data value will be (such as $Y = X + 3$, where 3 is a known constant). It is most efficient to use this constant immediately without having to find it in some memory location. Immediate instructions enable us to do this by including the data in the op-code itself.

All immediate instructions contain two bytes. The first byte is the op-code which tells what's to be done, the second byte is the data to be used. MVI A (Move Immediate) is an example of an immediate instruction.

Here is a review of the procedures you have learned so far. Until these procedures become second nature to you, you may want to refer back to this summary chart.

To Load a Program
1. Press # .
2. Enter a 6 digit address (040 100Q or higher).
3. Press / .
4. Type in data 3 digits at a time. You'll hear a soft beep every time you press a button, and a loud beep every time you press the third digit of a 3 digit byte.
5. Go to step 4 until finished.

To Run a Program
1. Press • and 6 and / .
2. Type a 6 digit starting address.
3. If you make a mistake, go back to step 1.
4. Press / .
5. Press 4 to start the program.

To Stop a Program

1. Press 0 and # at the same time.

To Examine a Program and Make Changes

1. Press # .
2. Type in a 6 digit starting address.
3. You'll see the data at that address in the data/register display —the rightmost three digits.
4. To examine the next address, press + .
5. To examine the previous address, press − .
6. If you see a byte that needs to be changed, press / , type in the new data byte, then press / again.
7. Continue examining memory to the end of the program.

THE ADD IMMEDIATE INSTRUCTION

The computer is expected to do arithmetic and it will indeed. Most people think in terms of addition, subtraction, multiplication, and division when they think of arithmetic. The computer, however, has only addition and subtraction in its instruction set. In your later programming, you will find that the computer can be made to multiply and divide with programming, using only the addition or subtraction instructions. One of the addition instructions is Add Immediate (ADI—op-code 306Q) which requires two bytes; remember that all immediate instructions require two bytes. The data in the second byte of the instruction is added to the accumulator.

Suppose we wish to add the octal numbers 101Q, 023Q, and 177Q. Using only immediate instructions, we could write:

1. MVI A,101
2. ADI 023
3. ADI 177
4. HLT

We wrote the above program using the mnemonic codes, or op-codes, followed by the data. The data (101Q) in the op-code MVI A,101 is called the *operand*. An operand gives information to be used with an instruction; it may be a data value, a memory address, a register, or other necessary information. In the op-code STA 040 200, the address 040 200Q is the operand.

Registers

Converting the previous op-codes to machine code for a program to be placed at 040 100Q, we have:

STEP	ADDRESS	CODE	INSTRUCTION	COMMENT
1	040 100	076	MVI A,101	Put first number in
	040 101	101		accumulator.
2	040 102	306	ADI 023	Add the second number to
	040 103	023		the accumulator and put the result in accumulator.
3	040 104	306	ADI 177	Add the third number to the
	040 105	177		accumulator and put the result in accumulator.
4	040 106	166	HLT	Stop – the answer is in the accumulator.

If you could see into the accumulator as each step of the program was executed, you would see:

STEP	ACCUMULATOR
1	101
2	124 (101Q + 023Q)
3	323 (124Q + 177Q)
4	323

Load the program into the computer beginning at address 040 100Q, check each location to make sure that the instruction has been entered correctly, and then run the program. Examine the accumulator. Does it contain the correct octal number?

In order to get a look at the *subtotal* after each step, rewrite the program placing HLT's after each step.

The program will look like:

STEP	ADDRESS	CODE	INSTRUCTION	COMMENT
1	040 100	076	MVI A,101	Put first number in register
	040 101	101		A.
	040 102	166	HLT	Stop to look at register A.
2	040 103	306	ADI 023	Add second number to A and
	040 104	023		put result in A.
	040 105	166	HLT	Stop to look at A.
3	040 106	306	ADI 177	Add third number to A and
	040 107	177		put result in A.
4	040 110	166	HLT	Halt.

Enter the new program, checking for errors, and run it beginning at 040 100Q. Do the numbers in the accumulator at each step agree with the ones shown on page 37?

The two previous programs illustrate an important idea that you should realize later when writing your own programs from scratch. Most operations using the accumulator, such as arithmetic instructions, place the answer or result back into the accumulator so that *the number or data in the accumulator before the instruction was executed, is lost.*

Let's put all the instructions we have learned so far into one program. We will use both the direct and immediate instructions from the chart below:

INSTRUCTION	CODE
STA	062
LDA	072
ADI	306
MVI A	076
HLT	166

Here's an outline of the program:

1. Move an octal number into the accumulator—MVI A.
2. Add a second number, immediate mode—ADI.
3. Store the sum into memory location #1, direct—STA.
4. Add a third number to the accumulator, direct mode—ADI.
5. Store that sum into memory location #2—STA.
6. Load the accumulator with the number from location #1.
7. Halt to examine the accumulator.
8. Load the accumulator with the number from location #2.
9. Halt to examine the accumulator.

This program is typical of many larger programs you'll be writing later. The program handles data and along the way, it stores partial results in memory locations for retrieval later.

Here's the program broken down into coded steps. You fill in the correct op-codes for each instruction. Fill in the blanks from memory (yours) and then check yourself, if necessary.

Registers

STEP	ADDRESS	CODE	INSTRUCTION	COMMENT
1	040 100 040 101	___ 111	MVI A,111	Put 111Q into register A.
2	040 102 040 103	___ 022	ADI 022	Add 022 to A.
3	040 104 040 105 040 106	___ 200 040	STA 040 200	Save the partial sum (111Q+022Q).
4	040 107 040 110	___ 135	ADI 135	Add 135 to A.
5	040 111 040 112 040 113	___ 201 040	STA 040 201	Save the final sum (111Q+022Q+135Q).
6	040 114 040 115 040 116	___ 200 040	LDA 040 200	Get the partial sum.
7	040 117	___	HLT	Stop to look at A.
8	040 120 040 121 040 122	___ 201 040	LDA 040 201	Get the final sum.
9	040 123	___	HLT	Stop to look at A.

Enter the program into the computer and run it. Record the values in the accumulator at each HLT.

    First HLT   _____   Sum of first two numbers.
    Second HLT   _____   Final result.

Completed program:

STEP	ADDRESS	CODE	INSTRUCTION	COMMENT
1	040 100 040 101	076 111	MVI A,111	Put 111Q into register A.
2	040 102 040 103	306 022	ADI 022	Add 022Q to A.
3	040 104 040 105 040 106	062 200 040	STA 040 200	Save the partial sum.

4	040 107	306	ADI 135	Add 135Q to A.
	040 110	135		
5	040 111	062	STA 040 201	Save the final sum.
	040 112	201		
	040 113	040		
6	040 114	072	LDA 040 200	Get the partial sum.
	040 115	200		
	040 116	040		
7	040 117	166	HLT	
8	040 120	072	LDA 040 201	Get the final sum.
	040 121	201		
	040 122	040		
9	040 123	166	HLT	

At the first HLT, the accumulator should contain 111Q + 022Q, which is 133Q. At the second HLT, the accumulator should contain 13Q + 135Q, which is 270Q.

SELF TEST

1. The accumulator is an example of: (circle one)
   a register,   an input/output port,   a memory location.

2. A computer program is placed in memory in:
   random order,   sequential order,   reverse order.

3. STA is the op-code for Store Accumulator. It is a:
   1 byte,   2 byte,   3 byte   instruction.

4. The starting address in memory where a program is stored:
   is always the same,   doesn't have to always be the same.

5. As a "debugging tool" many computers can step through a program one instruction at a time using the _____ _____ operation.

6. The LDA instruction uses three bytes. Byte two contains the _____-order address, byte three contains the _____-order address. (Fill in with the words "high" and "low.")

Registers

7. Mnemonic op-codes are used as shorthand for binary instructions because _____
   _____.

8. What is the purpose of a *breakpoint* in a program? _____
   _____.

9. What is the program counter? _____
   _____.

10. Here is a short machine language program using some of the instructions discussed in this section. Study the program, then answer the questions below.

STEP	ADDRESS	CODE	INSTRUCTION	COMMENT
1	040 100	076	MVI A,101	Move 101Q to
	040 101	101		accumulator.
2	040 102	062	STA 040 150	Store contents of A at
	040 103	150		address 040 150Q.
	040 104	040		
3	040 105	072	LDA 040 111	Load the accumulator
	040 106	111		with data byte at
	040 107	040		address 040 111Q.
4	040 110	166	HLT	Halt.
	040 111	202		Data stored at 040 111Q.

    After the program has run and reached the HLT,
    What are the contents of the accumulator? _____
    What are the contents of the address 040 150Q? _____
    What are the contents of the program counter?
    _____ _____

    What are the contents of the address 040 111Q? _____
    Did the contents of address 040 150Q change? _____
    Did the contents of address 040 111Q change? _____
    How many memory addresses does the above
      program occupy? _____

11. Fill in the blanks:

INSTRUCTION NAME	MNEMONIC	OCTAL OP-CODE
_____	MVI A	_____
_____	ADI	_____
_____	STA	_____
_____	LDA	_____
_____	HLT	_____

12. Identify the following instructions as either direct mode or immediate mode:
    MVI A _____
    ADI   _____
    STA   _____
    LDA   _____

13. Which of the above instructions must be followed by a data byte? _____ _____

14. Which of the above instructions must be followed by a memory address? _____ _____

15. If the accumulator contains 111Q and the STA instruction is executed, can we tell what the accumulator will contain afterwards? _____.

Chapter Five

Registers (MVI, MOV)

USING THE OTHER REGISTERS

We briefly mentioned registers in chapter four and stated that the accumulator was a register—register A. There are six other eight bit registers which are available for you to use when programming. These registers are often referred to by letter (B, C, D, E, H. L). In the octal op-code for a given instruction, however, they are referred to by a three bit code:

REGISTER	OCTAL	BINARY
B	0	000
C	1	001
D	2	010
E	3	011
H	4	100
L	5	101
A	7	111

If you will memorize the table above, you will find it easy to remember many of the octal instruction codes that refer to registers. You'll understand this better after reading the following section on the Move Immediate instruction.

MOVE IMMEDIATE—MVI

We used the MVI A instruction previously in connection with the accumulator—the octal code was 076Q. The MVI instruction can be used with any of the eight bit registers by using the format OX6, where *X* refers to the three bit code for the register being used. Substituting an octal number from the table above, the variations become:

MVI B would be 006Q,
MVI C would be 016Q,
MVI D would be 026Q,
MVI E would be 036Q,
MVI H would be 046Q,
MVI L would be 056Q,
and MVI A would be 076Q.

Therefore, you can see that data may be moved immediately into any register using the MVI instruction by changing the middle digit in the octal op-code. The MVI instruction always begins with *0* and always ends with *6*; the middle digit gives the register involved.

Many other instructions to be introduced later will use the same numbers 0 through 7 to represent a register. That is one reason why it's so convenient to use octal shorthand notation to represent the eight bit binary instructions.

Notice in the table on page 43 that the octal number 6Q is not listed to represent a register; the octal code *6* is used to represent the *data byte* at a particular memory location — referred to as *M*. Therefore, the octal op-code 066Q is a valid one and will be explained further in a later section. For now, we are concerned only with the registers.

Here's a program which will enter different values into each of the seven registers:

STEP	ADDRESS	CODE	INSTRUCTION	COMMENT
1	040 100 040 101	___ 000	MVI B,000	Move immediate to B, 000Q.
2	040 102 040 103	___ 011	MVI C,011	Move immediate to C, 011Q.
3	040 104 040 105	___ 022	MVI D,022	Move immediate to D, 022Q.
4	040 106 040 107	___ 033	MVI E,033	Move immediate to E, 033Q.
5	040 110 040 111	___ 044	MVI H,044	Move immediate to H, 044Q.

Registers   45

6	040 112	___	MVI L,055	Move immediate to L, 055Q.
	040 113	055		
7	040 114	___	MVI A,077	Move immediate to A, 077Q.
	040 115	077		
8	040 116	166	HLT	

Fill in the blanks above with the appropriate op-code, then enter the program into your computer and run it. Use the following procedure to record the results:

1. Press • 2 and record the values in the display.
   ___ ___ ___   ___ ___ ___   ___ ___

2. Press • 3 and record the values in the display.
   ___ ___ ___   ___ ___ ___   ___ ___

3. Press • 4 and record the values in the display.
   ___ ___ ___   ___ ___ ___   ___ ___

4. Press • 5 and record the values in the display.
   ___ ___ ___   ___ ___ ___   ___ ___

As you can see, any data byte can be moved into any register using the Move Immediate (MVI) instruction.

MOVE

In addition to moving data into a register, we can also move data from one register to another. Once again, the data is really *copied*, not moved. If the data is moved from register A to register B, for instance, the data in A remains unchanged. In this example, register A is called the *source* (origin of the data), and register B is called the *destination* (place to which the data is moved).

The *Move* instruction moves data from one register to another—the format for the instruction is:

$$1 \ D \ S$$

where D is the destination register, and S is the source register. The octal digits used for D and S are the same as those shown on page 43.

As an example, suppose we wish to move data from the accumulator (register A) to register B. Since the octal code for A is

7Q (111B) and the code for B is 0Q (000B) the instruction for Move register A to register B would be:

107Q   or   01000111B

The op-code would be written MOV B,A. Notice the order in which the two registers are written: the destination register is first, followed by the source register.

In general, the contents of any register can be moved to any other register using the MOV instruction. This is done by formatting the op-code as 1DS, where D is the destination register and S is the source register. Some examples are:

1 7 0   MOV A,B   Move to A, the data in register B.
1 1 2   MOV C,D   Move to C, the data in register D.
1 0 3   MOV B,E   Move to B, the data in register E.
1 5 7   MOV L,A   Move to L, the data in register A.
1 4 4   MOV H,H   Move to H, the data in register H.

Notice that most any combination of moves is possible; even the last example, which moves the contents of register H back into itself, is legal, although the instruction would serve no real purpose. Again, be sure to notice that the destination register is designated first in the op-code, and the source register is designated last.

Exercise: Fill in the code for each of the MOV or MVI instructions.
 1. MOV H,L ___ ___ ___
 2. MOV L,H ___ ___ ___
 3. MOV E,B ___ ___ ___
 4. MVI L,111 ___ ___ ___   ___ ___ ___
 5. MOV C,A ___ ___ ___
 6. MVI C,377 ___ ___ ___   ___ ___ ___
 7. MOV A,B ___ ___ ___

REGISTER ROLL

Moving data from one register to another can simulate the *roll* function for registers in a pocket calculator. Consider a roll-up of data in registers B, C, D, and E with the accumulator acting as a temporary storage place.

Registers

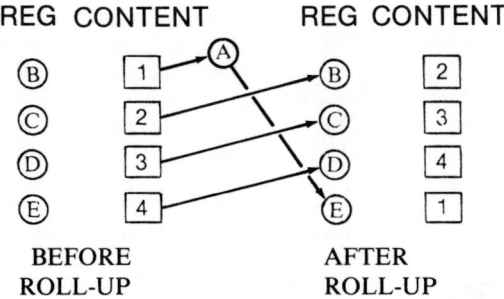

This could be done on the computer by:
1. Put 001 (1) into register B,
2. Put 002 (2) into register C,
3. Put 003 (3) into register D,
4. Put 004 (4) into register E,
} MVI R, data

5. Copy register B into register A,
6. Copy register C into register B,
7. Copy register D into register C,
8. Copy register E into register D,
9. Copy register A into register E.
} MOV R_1, R_2

The program shown below will perform the roll-up operation; we'll leave the roll-down operation for you to program. Notice that we've used the accumulator (register A) as a temporary *holding place* for the contents of register B until register E is copied. Thus no register has its contents destroyed until its contents are copied into another register.

Register Roll-Up

ADDRESS	CODE	INSTRUCTION	COMMENT
040 100	006	MVI B,001	Put 001 into register B.
040 101	001		
040 102	016	MVI C,002	Put 002 into register C.
040 103	002		
040 104	026	MVI D,003	Put 003 into register D.
040 105	003		
040 106	036	MVI E,004	Put 004 into register E.
040 107	004		
040 110	166	HLT	This Halt was put here so that you could check the register for correct values.

040 111	170	MOV A,B	Move to A, the contents of B.
040 112	101	MOV B,C	Move to B, the contents of C.
040 113	112	MOV C,D	Move to C, the contents of D.
040 114	123	MOV D,E	Move to D, the contents of E.
040 115	137	MOV E,A	Move to E, the contents of A.
040 116	116	HLT	Halt.

Exercise: Enter the program and run it — check each register when the program halts and fill in the blanks below:

REGISTER	BEFORE	AFTER
B	_____	_____
C	_____	_____
D	_____	_____
E	_____	_____

```
REG  CONTENT           REG  CONTENT
 Ⓑ     [1]              Ⓑ     [4]
 Ⓒ     [2]              Ⓒ     [1]
 Ⓓ     [3]              Ⓓ     [2]
 Ⓔ     [4]              Ⓔ     [3]
          [A]
  BEFORE                  AFTER
 ROLL-DOWN              ROLL-DOWN
```

Write the program to perform roll-down operation. Refer to the ten steps for roll-down given above.

ADDRESS	CODE	INSTRUCTION	COMMENT
040 100	_____	_____	_____
040 101	_____		
040 102	_____	_____	_____
040 103	_____		
040 104	_____	_____	_____
040 105	_____		
040 106	_____	_____	_____
040 107	_____		
040 110	_____	_____	_____
040 111	_____	_____	_____
040 112	_____	_____	_____
040 113	_____	_____	_____
040 114	_____	_____	_____
040 115	_____	_____	_____
040 116	_____	_____	_____

Registers

THE STACK

Many computers, and many calculators, use *stacks* to temporarily store data. A stack is usually a string of memory locations where one byte of data is pushed in at location number one, and each data byte is shifted down one in the string in order to make room for the new byte. Let's try a demonstration using registers instead of memory locations. Suppose there is a data byte in the accumulator which we want to save. There is also data in registers B, C, and D. We don't care what is in register E. Here's the picture:

	In the accumulator	1	save this
	in register B	2	save this
A *stack* of	in register C	3	save this
data in	in register D	4	save this
registers.	in register E	5	don't care about this

The data in the accumulator could be *pushed* on to the *stack* of registers by using the MOV instructions:

MOV R_1,R_2 { Move data in D to E, move data in C to D, move data in B to C, move data in A to B. }

Now we would have:

in the accumulator	1	same number stays
in register B	1	all *pushed down*
in register C	2	one register.
in register D	3	
in register E	4	
	5	is gone.

We can just as easily *pop* a data byte off the *stack* and into the accumulator, while moving the other values up one register.

BEFORE		AFTER	
A	1	A	2
B	2	B	3
C	3	C	4
D	4	D	5
E	5	E	5

This can be done with MOV instructions in this order:

> Move data in B to A,
> move data in C to B,
> move data in D to C,
> move data in E to D.

Notice the order in which the previous two examples were performed. Order is important. What would happen if we did this:

> Move data in E to D,
> move data in D to C,
> move data in C to B,
> move data in B to A.

Would the data be *popped* off the stack correctly?

Example: To illustrate the push and pop operations, we'll write a program to perform both operations, then put some sample data into the registers, and then step through the program. The program will push the data byte 377 from the accumulator onto the stack of registers, and then pop the value 377 back off the stack into the accumulator.

To review, the procedure for entering data directly into a register is as follows:
1. Press • .
2. Select a register by pressing the key with the register you wish to access in the upper left corner. Since all registers are accessed in pairs (AF, BC, DE, and HL) there are two registers designated on each key.
3. Press / .
4. Enter the value for the register. Note that you must enter the data in pairs—one data byte for each register. You may only be changing one register, so the other registers' contents must be repeated.
5. Press / again, *or* repeat the procedure from step 1 for each register into which you want to enter a value.

If the values are pre-loaded into the registers, the program becomes:

> { MOV H,E   Save the original value of E in H.
>   MOV E,D

Registers

```
        ⎧ MOV D,C
PUSH ⎨ MOV C,B
        ⎩ MOV B,A
          MVI A,000   Clear the accumulator
          HLT         Stop here to look at the registers.

        ⎧ MOV A,B
        ⎪ MOV B,C
POP  ⎨ MOV C,D
        ⎪ MOV D,E
        ⎩ MOV E,H
          HLT         Stop once more to look at each
                      register. Everyone back?
```

Here's the program:

ADDRESS	CODE	INSTRUCTION	COMMENT
040 100	143	MOV H,E	Move E to H.
040 101	132	MOV E,D	Move D to E.
040 102	121	MOV D,C	Move C to D.
040 103	110	MOV C,B	Move B to C.
040 104	107	MOV B,A	Move A to B.
040 105	076	MVI A,000	Put 000Q into register A.
040 106	000		
040 107	166	HLT	Halt.
040 110	170	MOV A,B	Move B to A.
040 111	101	MOV B,C	Move C to B.
040 112	112	MOV C,D	Move D to C.
040 113	123	MOV D,E	Move E to D.
040 114	134	MOV E,H	Move H to E.
040 115	166	HLT	Halt.

Enter the indicated values into the corresponding registers, then run the program and fill in the blanks below:

	ENTRIES MADE BEFORE RUN	CONTENTS AT FIRST HALT	AT SECOND HALT
Register A	377	___	___
Register B	001	___	___
Register C	002	___	___
Register D	003	___	___
Register E	004	___	___

Chapter Six

Registers
(ADD, SUB, INR, DCR)

ADD REGISTER AND SUBTRACT REGISTER

Two instructions commonly used for register arithmetic are the Add Register (ADD R) and the Subtract Register (SUB R) instructions. Both use the octal register code to designate which register's contents are to be added to or subtracted from the accumulator. The register code is the same one used previously for the MVI and MOV instructions. Here is a table of octal codes for each of the Add and Subtract instructions:

ADD REGISTER		SUBTRACT REGISTER	
Add B to A	200	Subtract B from A	220
Add C to A	201	Subtract C from A	221
Add D to A	202	Subtract D from A	222
Add E to A	203	Subtract E from A	223
Add H to A	204	Subtract H from A	224
Add L to A	205	Subtract L from A	225
Add A to A	207	Subtract A from A	227

Notice that all ADD R instructions have the format 20X, and all subtract instructions have the format 22X, where the third digit in each op-code is the register holding the value to be added or subtracted from the accumulator. When the instruction is executed, the result is put into the accumulator. For example, if the accumulator holds the value 111Q and register C contains the value 222Q and the ADD C instruction is executed, then the accumulator's contents become 333Q.

An illustration of the ADD C instruction:

```
BEFORE EXECUTION                    AFTER EXECUTION
    OF ADD C                           OF ADD C
    1 1 1   ————▶  Register A  ————▶   3 3 3
    2 2 2   ————▶  Register C  ————▶   2 2 2
```

Note that the contents of register C remain the same. Of course, any of the registers could be used in place of C by changing the third digit of the op-code; the accumulator can even be added to itself using op-code 227.

The Subtract instruction works in exactly the same manner, with the value of the designated register being subtracted from the accumulator, and the result being put into the accumulator. If you use the Subtract Register A (SUB A) instruction, the accumulator will be set to zero—thus you have a quick way to clear the accumulator.

Here is an example of the use of ADD R and SUB R. The table shows the original contents of each register, and then the change in the *accumulator* as each of the four instructions is executed. Pay special attention to step 3.

	Reg B	Reg C	Reg D	Reg A
0. Originally	003	002	007	377
1. SUB A	003	002	007	000
2. ADD B	003	002	007	003
3. ADD D	003	002	007	012
4. SUB C	003	002	007	010

INCREMENT REGISTER AND DECREMENT REGISTER

The data in the registers themselves may be altered by use of the Increment Register (INR R) and Decrement Register (DCR R) instructions. Registers are often used as counters in programs where some operation is repeated a given number of times. The Increment Register instruction is used to increase a count by one. As in some of the previous instructions you've learned, the INR and DCR instructions use the octal register code (0 to 7) to specify which register is being incremented or decremented. The INR instruction has the format 0X4Q where the middle digit specifies the register being incremented. For instance, the op-code 074Q translates to INR A, or increment accumulator. The

Registers

DCR instruction has the format 0X5Q; again, the middle digit specifies the decremented register. As an example, 005Q would mean decrement register B by one.

INR R = 0X4	DCR R = 0X5
REGISTER	CODE
A	7
B	0
C	1
D	2
E	3
H	4
L	5

Let's construct a program which will count up in one register, add the final sum to another register, and then count down in the second register.

Here's the procedure:

SUB A	Clear the accumulator
MOV B,A	Clear register B
INR B	Count equals 1
INR B	Count equals 2
INR B	Count equals 3
MOV C,B	Move the final count (3) into C
DCR C	Count equals 2
DCR C	Count equals 1
DCR C	Count equals 0
ADD B	Add B to the accumulator
ADD C	Add C to the accumulator
HLT	Stop

The Counting Program

ADDRESS	CODE	INSTRUCTION	COMMENT
040 100	227	SUB A	Subtract A from A. (Set A to 0.)
040 101	107	MOV B,A	Move A to B. (Set B to 0.)
040 102	004	INR B	B = 1
040 103	004	INR B	B = 2
040 104	004	INR B	B = 3
040 105	110	MOV C,B	Move B to C. (C now equals 3.)

040 106	015	DCR C	C = 2	
040 107	015	DCR C	C = 1	
040 110	015	DCR C	C = 0	
040 111	200	ADD B	A = 0 + 3 = 3	
040 112	201	ADD C	A = 3 + 0 = 3	
040 113	166	HLT	Halt — end of program.	

Exercise: Enter the counting program into the computer and run it, then record the values indicated in the tables below:

REGISTER	CONTENTS
A	_____
B	_____
C	_____

SELF TEST

1. Which instruction will move a data byte into a specified register? _____

2. Fill in the blanks with the octal digit that corresponds to each register:

REGISTER	OCTAL DIGIT
A	7
B	_____
C	_____
D	_____
E	_____
H	_____
L	_____

3. Which instruction will transfer the contents of one register to another register? _____

4. The ADD instruction will add the contents of a specified register to the accumulator. Where does the sum of the two registers end up? _____

5. Is the same true of the SUB (subtract) instruction? _____

Registers

6. Which instruction will add *1* to a specified register?
   _____

7. Which instruction will subtract *1* from a specified register?
   _____

8. If register B contains 003Q and you decrement it four times, what value will be in B? _____

SECTION TWO

Chapter Seven

Introduction

In the previous section you learned to use some of the basic 8080 machine language instructions in short programs. You are now familiar with the operation of the H8 front panel. In this section, you will write many short programs yourself; therefore, we will present a review of the instructions covered so far, as well as the symbolism and format used to describe them.

The instructions discussed in Section One can be classified according to the addressing mode used. There are three general classes: direct, immediate, and register.

Direct instructions require three bytes. The first byte designates the instruction; the other two bytes provide the address of the memory location where data is to be found or where data is to be placed. You've learned two direct instructions so far:

Load Accumulator	LDA addr	072
		nnn
		mmm
Store Accumulator	STA addr	062
		nnn
		mmm

(Throughout the book we'll be using mmm nnn to represent a general octal address.)

Immediate instructions require two bytes. The first byte designates the instruction, and the second byte provides the data which is to be used. You've learned two instructions of the immediate type:

Add Immediate	ADI data	306
		XXX
Move Immediate	MVI data	0D6
		XXX

(An octal number between 0 and 7 is substituted for D depending on which register is to receive the data XXX.)

Register instructions require only one byte. This byte designates the operation to be performed, as well as which register(s) are involved. You've learned five register instructions so far:

Add Register	ADD R	20S
Subtract Register	SUB R	22S
Increment Register	INR R	0D4
Decrement Register	DCR R	0D5
Move	MOV R_1,R_2	1DS

(An octal number, 0 to 7, is substituted for D or S depending on which register is required.)

In addition to the instructions above, you have learned one control instruction—HLT, which is used to stop operation of the computer.

Here is a table of instructions used so far:

Table 1

NAME	MNEMONIC	OP-CODE	CLASS	NO. OF BYTES
Load Accumulator	LDA	072	Direct	3
Store Accumulator	STA	062	Direct	3
Add Immediate	ADI data	306	Immediate	2
Move Immediate	MVI R,data	0D6	Immediate	2
Add Register	ADD R	20S	Register	1
Subtract Register	SUB R	22S	Register	1
Increment Register	INR R	0D4	Register	1
Decrement Register	DCR R	0D5	Register	1
Move Register	MOV R_1,R_2	1DS	Register	1
Halt	HLT	166	Control	1

Note: D in Op-Code for Destination register
S in Op-Code for Source register

Introduction

For octal values substituted for D and S, see Table 2, below.

Table 2

REGISTER (R)	OCTAL CODE (D or S)
A	7
B	0
C	1
D	2
E	3
H	4
L	5

Assuming you have studied the first section and you understand how these instructions work, we will build on that foundation adding new instructions as we go.

Chapter Eight

Flowcharts, Counters (JMP, SUI, NOP)

THE JUMP INSTRUCTION

The programs which you have used so far have been written to operate sequentially — that is, each instruction is executed one at a time, in order, according to address. The program shown below is typical of this type program:

ADDRESS	CODE	INSTRUCTION	COMMENT
040 100	006	MVI B,001	Move 001Q into register B.
040 101	001		
040 102	016	MVI C,002	Move 002Q into register C.
040 103	002		
040 104	171	MOV A,C	Move the contents of C to A.
040 105	110	MOV C,B	Move the contents of B to C.
040 106	107	MOV B,A	Move the contents of A to B.
040 107	166	HLT	Halt operation.

In the above program the instruction at address 040 100Q is executed first, then the one at 040 102Q,
               then the one at 040 104Q,
               then the one at 040 105Q,
               then the one at 040 106Q,
          and then the one at 040 107.

This normal sequential operation of the program can be altered by a group of instructions called branch instructions. One of the simplest and most useful of this group is the jump instruction.

The Jump instruction (JMP) alters the order of program execution by replacing the contents of the program counter. Remember that the program counter is normally incremented as each instruction is fetched so that it will point to the next sequentially addressed instruction. The jump instruction alters this normal sequence by replacing the address in the program counter with the address of the instruction you wish to execute next.

The JMP instruction is composed of three bytes—the first byte specifies the instruction, the second and third bytes tell the address you wish the program to jump *to*. The address specified in bytes two and three is placed in the program counter.

The format of the jump instruction is: 303
nnn
mmm

The address mmm nnn is placed in the program counter. The easiest way to learn the power of the JMP instruction is to use it in a program.

The following program uses three instructions. The first one merely clears the accumulator—it subtracts the contents of the accumulator from itself; $A - A = 0$. The second instruction increments the accumulator; $A = A + 1$. The third instruction is a jump back to the second instruction. Therefore, instructions two and three will be repeated over and over again, and the contents of the accumulator will increase by one on each cycle until the program is stopped.

Load this short program into the computer:

ADDRESS	CODE	INSTRUCTION	COMMENT
040 100	227	SUB A	Clears the accumulator.
040 101	074	INR R	Increments the accumulator.
040 102	303 101 040	JMP 040 101	Jump to instruction at address 040 101Q.

Set the program counter to 040 100Q and leave the display set to PC. Single-step through the program and check the values of the PC in the display at each step.

Flowcharts, Counters

```
PRESS KEYS                      DISPLAY READS
1.  •    6   /   0 4 0  1 0 0  /    0 4 0   1 0 0   P C
2.  7                                0 4 0   1 0 1   P C
3.  7                                0 4 0   1 0 2   P C
4.  7                                0 4 0   1 0 1   P C
5.  7                                0 4 0   1 0 2   P C
6.  7                                0 4 0   1 0 1   P C
```

The display shows that the program is proceeding from address 040 101Q to 040 102Q to 040 101Q to 040 102Q...over and over again. This is called a *loop*.

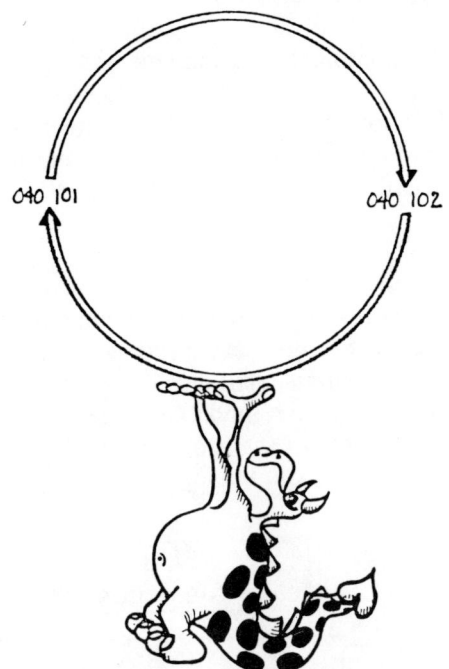

In other words, the program is looping.

Reset the program counter to 040 100Q and set the display to AF. Single-step through the program again and check the values in the accummulator at each step. (Ignore register F for now.)

```
PRESS KEYS                      DISPLAY READS
1.  •   6   /   0 4 0  1 0 0  /    0 4 0   1 0 0   P C
2.  •   2                            X X X   X X X   A F
```

3. 7   0 0 0 X X X A F
4. 7   0 0 1 X X X A F
5. 7   0 0 1 X X X A F
6. 7   0 0 2 X X X A F
7. 7   0 0 2 X X X A F
8. 7   0 0 3 X X X A F
9. and so on...

At step 3, the accumulator is cleared to zero;
at step 4, the accumulator is incremented;
at step 5, the jump is executed;
at step 6, the accumulator is incremented again;
at step 7, the jump is executed again;
at step 8, the accumulator is incremented again,
and so on....

The three leftmost digits in the display show the value in the accumulator and confirm that it is being incremented each time the JMP instruction loops back to address 040 101.

FLOW CHARTS

A flow chart is a way to follow the logic in a program. It is an important concept, as most programs originate from a flow chart. In most flow charts, the logic of the program is broken down into steps, or blocks, and the blocks are connected by lines indicating the flow of the program logic. For the program we are currently working on, the logic diagram (or flow chart) is a simple one:

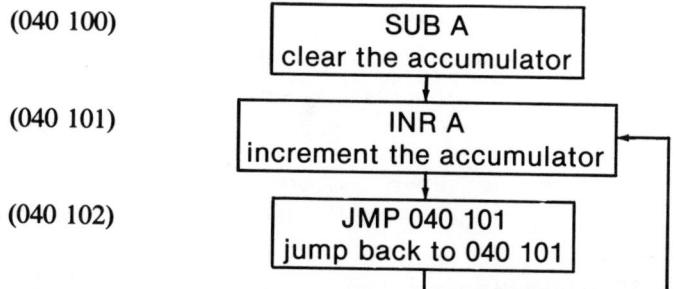

If the program was allowed to run, the accumulator would be incrementing faster than we could watch the results. By inserting a HLT in the loop, the value in the accumulator can be observed at each pass of the loop.

Flowcharts, Counters

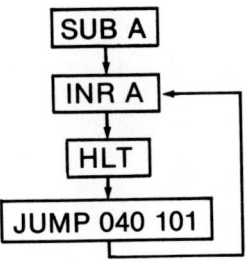

ADDRESS	CODE	INSTRUCTION	COMMENT
040 100	227	SUB A	Clear the accumulator.
040 101	074	INR A	Increment accumulator.
040 102	166	HLT	Stop here to observe accumulator.
040 103	303	JMP 040 101	Jump back to address 040 101Q.
040 104	101		
040 105	040		

To use the program,

```
PRESS KEY                          DISPLAY READS
1.  •   6   /   0 4 0   1 0 0  /   0 4 0   1 0 0   P C
2.  4                              X X X   X X X   A F
3.  4                              0 0 0   X X X   A F
4.  4                              0 0 1   X X X   A F
5.  4                              0 0 2   X X X   A F
6.  4                              0 0 3   X X X   A F
7.  4                              0 0 4   X X X   A F
8.  4                              0 0 5   X X X   A F
```

Holding the 4 key down causes it to repeat, so you can watch the accumulator count up. Notice that after it reaches 377Q, the count goes back to zero and starts over.

Using the program, complete the trace below by filling in the blanks. Set the display to registers AF, and ignore the data that appears for register F.

ADDRESS	CODE	INSTRUCTION	P C	A F
040 100	227	SUB A	040 101	000 XXX
040 101	074	INR A	040 102	001 XXX
040 102	166	HLT	040 103	001 XXX
040 103	303	JMP 040 101	040 101	001 XXX
040 101	074	INR A	040 102	002 XXX
040 102	166	HLT	040 103	002 XXX
040 103	303	JMP 040 101	_____	_____

040 101	074	INR A	_____	_____
040 102	166	HLT	_____	_____
040 103	303	JMP 040 101	_____	_____
040 101	074	INR A	_____	_____
040 102	166	HLT	_____	_____

Filling in the traces step-by-step is a tedious job, but a good understanding of the program counter and registers will make your future programming a lot easier.

Exercise: You could change the last program to make it count by twos by inserting a second INR instruction:

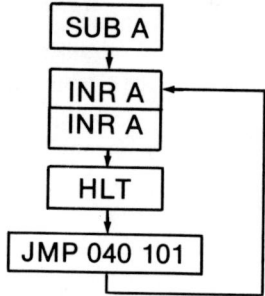

Here's the new program:

ADDRESS	CODE	INSTRUCTION
040 100	227	SUB A
040 101	074	INR A
040 102	074	INR A
040 103	166	HLT
040 104	303	JMP 040 101
040 105	101	
040 106	040	

Enter the program into memory and run it with the display set to AF. Then single-step with the display set to AF. Then single-step with the display set to PC.

Complete the following trace of the program:

ADDRESS	CODE	INSTRUCTION	P C	A F
040 100	227	SUB A	040 101	000 XXX
040 101	074	INR A	040 102	001 XXX
040 102	074	INR A	040 103	002 XXX
040 103	166	HLT	040 104	002 XXX
040 104	303	JMP 040 101	040 101	002 XXX

Flowcharts, Counters

040 101	074	INR A	040 102	003 XXX
040 102	074	INR A	040 103	004 XXX
040 103	166	HLT	040 104	004 XXX
040 104	303	JMP 040 101	040 101	004 XXX
040 101	074	INR A	_____	_____
040 102	074	INR A	_____	_____
040 103	166	HLT	_____	_____
040 104	303	JMP 040 101	_____	_____
040 101	074	INR A	_____	_____
040 102	074	INR A	_____	_____
040 103	166	HLT	_____	_____
040 104	303	JMP 040 101	_____	_____

As a further exercise, rewrite the program using ADI 002Q instead of two INR A instructions. Then write a program that counts by *threes* using the INR A instruction.

The previous programs all started at zero and counted upward. Suppose you want to begin counting at some point other than zero. In the original program the instruction SUB A was used to clear the accumulator. If you wish to begin counting from some other number, the MVI A (Move Immediate to Accumulator) instruction can be substituted for SUB A. Suppose you wish to start the count at 100Q and count upward by ones. The program would be:

ADDRESS	CODE	INSTRUCTION	COMMENT
040 100	076	MVI A,100	Move 100Q into register A.
040 101	100		
040 102	074	INR A	Increment register A.
040 103	166	HLT	Stop to examine A.
040 104	303	JMP 040 102	Jump back to 040 102Q.
040 105	102		
040 106	040		

Exercise: Fill in the trace of the above program showing the value in the accumulator at each HLT. Ignore the values in register F.

1st HLT	____ XXX AF
2nd HLT	____ XXX AF
3rd HLT	____ XXX AF
4th HLT	____ XXX AF

Draw a flowchart for the program.

You should keep in mind that there are several ways in which data can be loaded into the accumulator. In the last program, the original number was put into the accumulator with the MVI A instruction. Data can be loaded from a memory location using the LDA instruction as follows:

ADDRESS	CODE	INSTRUCTION	COMMENT
040 100	072	LDA 040 200	Load the accumulator with the data
040 101	200		at address 040 200Q.
040 102	040		
040 103	074	INR A	Increment the accumulator.
040 104	166	HLT	Stop to look at register A.
040 105	303	JMP 040 103	Jump back to 040 103Q.
040 106	103		
040 107	040		

The starting number must be placed at memory location 040 200 before the program is run.

Exercise: Write a program to count by one, beginning with the number stored at address 040 200Q. (Use ADI 001Q, not INR A.)

ADDRESS	CODE	INSTRUCTION	COMMENT
040 100	___	_____	_____
040 101	___	_____	_____
040 102	___	_____	_____
_____	___	_____	_____
_____	___	_____	_____

Exercise: Write two programs which count by twos:
  a. One program should begin counting at 100 (using MVI A).
  b. The other should begin counting from the number stored at location 040 200Q (store 100Q at address 040 200Q).
Write two programs which count down by ones:
  a. One program should count down from 100 (using MVI A).
  b. The other should count down beginning from the number stored at address 040 200Q (store 100Q at 040 200Q).

SUBTRACT IMMEDIATE

In section one you learned the ADI (Add Immediate) instruction. In the next program we'll introduce the companion in-

Flowcharts, Counters

struction—Subtract Immediate (SUI). The SUI instruction subtracts one data byte from the accumulator and puts the result in the accumulator. The SUI instruction, therefore, requires two bytes just as ADI does. The second byte is the data byte to be subtracted from the accumulator. (Remember that the original contents of the accumulator will be lost.)

Here's a program which will count down by twos, starting from 100Q:

ADDRESS	CODE	INSTRUCTION	COMMENT
040 100	076	MVI A,100	Put 100Q into register A.
040 101	100		
040 102	326	SUI 002	Subtract 002Q from register A and
040 103	002		put the result in A.
040 104	166	HLT	Stop to examine A.
040 105	303	JMP 040 102	Jump back to 040 102Q.
040 106	102		
040 107			

Load the program into the computer and run it. Using the 4 key, record the values in the accumulator at each HLT as the computer loops through the program.

HALT	ACCUMULATOR
1st HLT	_____
2nd HLT	_____
3rd HLT	_____
4th HLT	_____
5th HLT	_____

Again, ignore register F for now.

MORE COUNTING

In section one you were introduced to the INR (Increment Register) and DCR (Decrement Register) instructions. Remember that either instruction may be used with any of the registers, as follows:

INR is 0 D 4   where D is an octal digit from 0 to 7.
DCR is 0 D 5   where D is an octal digit from 0 to 7.

Decrement register B would be 005Q.
Increment register A would be 074Q.
And now, here is a program that will count upward by ones in register B:

ADDRESS	CODE	INSTRUCTION	COMMENT
040 100	006	MVI B,000	Move 000Q into register B.
040 101	000		
040 102	004	INR B	Increment register B.
040 103	166	HLT	Stop to look at register B.
040 104	303	JMP 040 102	Jump back to 040 102Q.
040 105	102		
040 106	040		

Enter the program into your computer and then set the display to register pair BC.

Single step through the program, checking the program counter and register B at each step. Complete the program trace below as you go:

ADDRESS	INSTRUCTION	REG. B	PROGRAM COUNTER
040 100	MVI B,000	000	040 102
040 102	INR B	001	040 103
040 103	HLT	001	040 104
040 104	JMP 040 102	001	040 102
040 102	INR B	___	___
040 103	HLT	___	___
040 104	JMP 040 102	___	___
040 102	INR B	___	___
040 103	HLT	___	___
040 104	JMP 040 102	___	___

and so on...

The exercise you have just completed should convince you that register B is incremented each time the *loop* in the program is executed. Notice that, as usual, the program counter always points to the next instruction to be executed.

Exercise: Modify the program so that the counter will be made to count in register C.

Flowcharts, Counters

```
MVI B,000 ←┐
INR B  ←───┴──→ (Change these two instructions)
HLT
JMP 040 102
```

Now run the program using the GO command key, with the display set to BC, and complete the following:

	DISPLAY
1st Halt	_____
2nd Halt	_____
3rd Halt	_____
4th Halt	_____
5th Halt	_____
6th Halt	_____
7th Halt	_____

Exercise: Write a program to count up in both D *and* E registers at the same time. When you run the program using the procedure below, this is what *should* be displayed in the register D and E displays:

```
.  6  /  040 100  /     040 100 P C
4                       X X X  X X X  D E
4                       0 0 1  0 0 1  D E
4                       0 0 2  0 0 2  D E
4                       0 0 3  0 0 3  D E
4                       0 0 4  0 0 4  D E
4                       0 0 5  0 0 5  D E
```
and so on...

Notice that on the last program, both registers D and E seemed to change values at once when you hit the *GO* key. The computer is controlled by a clock which runs very fast. The computer completes each step in the program so fast that they appear to happen all at once; the computer *does* perform each step one at a time, however, just as the program tells it to do.

Exercise: Write a program to count up in register H, and down in register L. Only minor changes to the previous program are needed, and as a hint, (reg. H) + (reg. L) = 377Q. This is what the displays should look like:

```
  •     6   /   0 4 0   1 0 0   /      0 4 0   1 0 0   P C
  4                                    X X X   X X X   H L
  4                                    0 0 1   3 7 6   H L
  4                                    0 0 2   3 7 5   H L
  4                                    0 0 3   3 7 4   H L
  4                                    0 0 4   3 7 3   H L
  4                                    0 0 5   3 7 2   H L
and so on...
```

Exercise:
 a. Write a program to count up by twos in register B, starting from 000Q.
 b. Write a program to count up by twos in register C, starting from 000Q.
 c. Write a program to count down by twos in register C, starting from 377Q.

You should now be pretty good at writing machine language programs that count both forward and backward. The techniques you have learned will be very useful in your future programming.

You also know how to use the computer to generate a string of increasing integers (1, 2, 3, 4,...). It would be interesting to investigate the partial sums of these integers (1, 1+2, 1+2+3, 1+2+3+4,...). The partial sums can be created by generating the integers in one register, adding them in the accumulator, and saving the results in another register. In this next program, we'll use register C to generate the integers, and register B to hold the partial sums. Of course the addition is performed in the accumulator. Here is one way to do it:

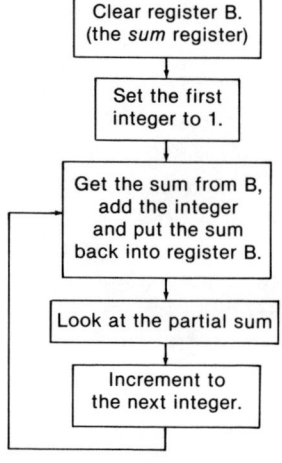

Flowcharts, Counters

ADDRESS	CODE	INSTRUCTION	COMMENT
040 100	006	MVI B,000	Clear register B.
040 101	000		
040 102	016	MVI C,001	Set the first integer = 1.
040 103	001		
040 104	170	MOV A,B	This gets the sum from B, adds the
040 105	201	ADD C	integer and stores the sum back
040 106	107	MOV B,A	into B.
040 107	166	HLT	Stop to look at BC (partial sum in B).
040 110	014	INR C	Increment new integer.
040 111	000	NOP	No operation. ← NEW INSTRUCTION
040 112	303	JMP 040 104	Go back to add new integer.
040 113	104		
040 114	040		

NO OPERATION (NOP)

The No Operation instruction does nothing—sound pretty useful? Actually it's a very handy instruction. NOPs are often put in so that new instructions can be added to the program at a later time.

Single-step through the program and complete the trace:

```
PRESS KEYS                            DISPLAY READS
  •   6   /   0 4 0   1 0 0   /     0 4 0   1 0 0   P C
  •   3                              X X X   X X X   B C
  4                                  _____       B C
  4                                  _____       B C
  4                                  _____       B C
  4                                  _____       B C
```
and so on...

Exercise: You know how to write a program that counts up in a register by twos, and you know how to start the count at any number using the MVI R instruction. Use this knowledge to write a program which will generate a string of positive, odd integers (1, 3, 5, 7,...) in register D. Use the instructions

MVI D
INR D
HLT
and JMP

Exercise: Now write a program which will generate the partial sums of the odd integers $(1, 1+3, 1+3+5, \ldots)$. Use register E to generate the odd integers $(1, 3, 5, 7, \ldots)$. Use register D to hold the partial sums $1, 1+3, 1+3+5, \ldots)$.

Hint: Register changes in the program on page 74 may accomplish the task. You will need to insert an instruction where the NOP was used.

Chapter Nine

PAM-8 Subroutines (BEEP, DELAY, CALL, RETURN)

USING THE PAM-8 SUBROUTINES

The Heathkit front panel monitor (PAM-8) has several subroutines that you may *call on* to perform particular functions. Two of them are called BEEP and DELAY. A subroutine is a short program which is used by a larger main program to perform a needed function. At the end of the subroutine, the program counter returns where it left off in the main program:

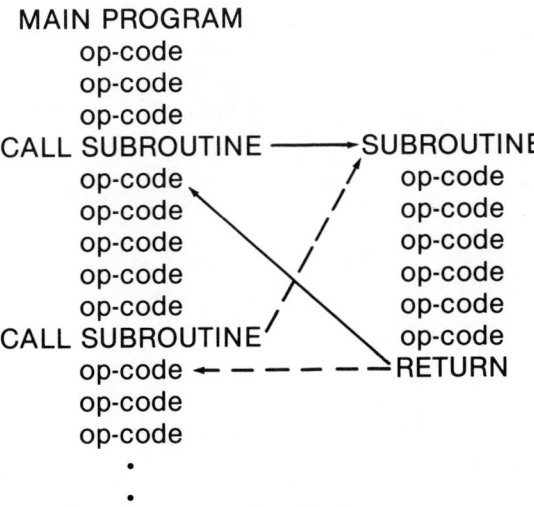

THE CALL INSTRUCTION

The CALL instruction belongs to the Branch instruction group, along with JUMP. In addition to changing the value of the program counter, the current memory location is saved so that the computer will know where to return when the subroutine is finished. The CALL instruction is always followed (sometime later in the subroutine) by the RETURN instruction. When the RETURN instruction is encountered the program counter is changed back to the address following the CALL. All this was illustrated above.

Notice that for each CALL instruction, there must be a RETURN instruction. That's the big difference between JUMPING to an address and CALLING an address—if you CALL an address, then you intend to return where you left off. Note that the subroutine performs the same function each time it is called.

THE BEEP

The PAM-8 subroutines stored in ROM memory along with the PAM-8 monitor are there for you to use. The BEEP sub-

PAM-8 Subroutines

routine is located at address 002 140Q and it is simply a short program that produces a *beep* tone when called.

Here's a program which uses the BEEP subroutine:

ADDRESS	CODE	INSTRUCTION	COMMENT
040 100	076	MVI A,100	Move 100Q into the accumulator.
040 101	100		
040 102	315	CALL 002 140	Call the BEEP subroutine.
040 103	140		
040 104	002		
040 105	166	HLT	Stop.
040 106	303	JMP	Jump back to repeat the beep.
040 107	100		
040 110	040		

The number stored in the accumulator when BEEP is called determines the length of the beep tone. The larger the number, the longer the tone.

Exercise:
a. Load the program into the computer and run it. Press 4 a few times to repeat the tone.
b. Now go back and store 050Q at location 040 101Q. Run the program and notice the beep is shorter.
c. Try 200Q and then 377Q at location 040 101Q.

In the previous exercise, which value in the accumulator gave the shortest beep? Which value gave the longest? What do you think would happen if you put 000Q into the accumulator? Try it. When the program is run you will still hear a beep. We didn't mean to trick you — all programs that are run use a *built-in* subroutine which will beep when the program halts. Up to now, you've actually been hearing two beeps; we CALL one, and the other is automatic when the H8 HLTs. They are so close together that they sound like one tone. Therefore, regardless of how small a value you put in the accumulator, you will hear a beep. You can make the beep longer than the automatic one, but not shorter.

Exercise: You learned previously about the NOP (No Operation) instruction. Try putting a NOP at address 040 105Q in the previous program in place of the HLT. BEWARE! It will be noisy. To stop it press 0 and # together. With the NOP in the program in place of the HLT, there is nothing to stop it from running and the computer cycles so fast that it sounds like it's producing one long BEEEEEEEEEP.

The BEEP subroutine is a handy one that you can call on in your later programming whenever an audio tone is desired.

THE DELAY

Another useful subroutine is the time delay. It can be called on to make the computer wait a specified time between instructions. Up to now we've been doing delays by inserting a HLT where we wanted a delay, and then pressing 4 to get started again. The DELAY subroutine will simply wait a certain length of time, and then continue executing the rest of the program. As you well know, the computer executes instructions *very* fast, so it's nice to have a subroutine to call on that will slow things down. The length of the delay is determined by the value in accumulator when the subroutine is called; the larger the number, the longer the delay.

A good way to illustrate this problem might be to look at the previous program. With the NOP in the program, the computer produces what sounds like one long continuous tone, but it is really a series of shorter tones sounded with (practically) no space between them. In the program that follows, we have put a DELAY between each tone:

ADDRESS	CODE	INSTRUCTION	COMMENT
040 100	076	MVI A,100	Put 100Q into the accumulator. (This
040 101	100		sets the length of tone.)
040 102	315	CALL 002 140	CALL 002 140Q for BEEP.
040 103	140		
040 104	002		
040 105	076	MVI A,100	Put 100Q into the accumulator. (This
040 106	100		sets the length of delay.)
040 107	315	CALL 000 053	CALL 000 053Q for DELAY.
040 110	053		
040 111	000		
040 112	076	MVI A,100	Put 100Q into the accumulator. (Set
040 113	100		length of tone.)
040 114	315	CALL 002 140	CALL 002 140Q for BEEP.
040 115	140		
040 116	002		
040 117	166	HLT	Stop.

PAM-8 Subroutines

The program above will produce two short tones, with a delay between them. Load it into the computer and run it.

Exercise:
a. Replace locations 040 112Q through 040 117Q with:

ADDRESS	CODE	INSTRUCTION
040 112	303	JMP 040 100
040 113	100	
040 114	040	
040 115	000	NOP
040 116	000	NOP
040 117	000	NOP

Now run the program and be prepared to stop it with:
0   #
What happened? _____
_____.

b. Change the BEEP tone length at location 040 101Q from 100Q to 200Q and then run the program.
Describe the results: _____
_____.

c. Change the DELAY time at location 040 106Q from 100Q to 377Q, then run the program and describe the result:
_____
_____.

Up to now, the DELAY length and BEEP tone length have been put into the accumulator using the MVI A instruction. Another way to load the accumulator with a known value is to have a number in one of the other registers (B, C, D, etc.) and then use the MOV instruction to transfer it to the accumulator. The program could be re-written:

ADDRESS	CODE	INSTRUCTION	COMMENT
040 100	170	MOV A,B	Move to A, the contents of B.
040 101	315	CALL 002 140	CALL BEEP.
040 102	140		
040 103	002		
040 104	171	MOV A,C	Move to A, the contents of C.
040 105	315	CALL 000 053	CALL DELAY.
040 106	053		
040 107	000		

```
040 110    303    JMP 040 100    Jump to address 040 100Q.
040 111    100
040 112    040
```

Load the program into the computer and run it. Don't forget to load registers B and C with some value before running the program—use values such as 100Q or other values previously used.

A third way to set BEEP and DELAY lengths is to load the accumulator with the contents of a memory location. In the program shown below, memory locations 040 117Q and 040 120Q hold the values to be put into the accumulator:

ADDRESS	CODE	INSTRUCTION	COMMENT
040 100	072	LDA 040 117	Load the accumulator with the data
040 101	117		byte at address 040 117Q.
040 102	040		
040 103	315	CALL 002 140	CALL BEEP subroutine.
040 104	140		
040 105	002		
040 106	072	LDA 040 120	Load the accumulator with the data
040 107	120		byte at address 040 120Q.
040 110	040		
040 111	315	CALL 000 053	CALL DELAY subroutine.
040 112	053		
040 113	000		
040 114	303	JMP 040 100	Jump to address 040 100Q.
040 115	100		
040 116	040		

Again, load the program into memory and run it. Be sure to store known values at memory locations 040 117Q and 040 120Q. You can see that there are usually several different ways to accomplish a task in machine language. The result is the same, but some programs conserve memory space, or maybe run faster. There isn't necessarily a right or wrong way to write a particular program.

The time DELAY subroutine can be applied to the counting programs you learned back in Chapter Six. In the previous counting programs, the HLT instruction was used to stop and view the display. We can now put in a time delay which is long enough to allow us to see the counter in action. Any of the registers except register A can be used for counting—register A

PAM-8 Subroutines

is needed for the DELAY subroutine. We will use register C in the example below. Note that we also zero register B for use later, if desired.

ADDRESS	CODE	INSTRUCTION	COMMENT
040 100	227	SUB A	Clear the accumulator.
040 101	107	MOV B,A	Clear register B.
040 102	117	MOV C,A	Clear register C.
040 103	076	MVI A,XXX	Set the length of DELAY.
040 104	XXX		
040 105	315	CALL 000 053	Call the DELAY subroutine.
040 106	053		
040 107	000		
040 110	014	INR C	Increment register C.
040 111	000	NOP	
040 112	303	JMP 040 103	
040 113	103		
040 114	040		

An octal number of your choice should be placed at address 040 104Q in order to set the DELAY length.

Exercise:
   a. Run the program in your computer, placing a number at 040 104Q which allows you to read the display without strain.
   b. Change the program to make it count up in register B, instead of register C.
   c. Change the program to make it count up in registers B and C at the same time (both 1, both 2, both 3, etc.).
   d. Change the program to make it count up by twos in register C.
   e. Change the program to make it count up in register C, and down in register B, at the same time.

In Chapter Eight, you ran many programs using the display, with HLT's in the programs to stop the display. If you have time, go back to those programs and insert the DELAY subroutine in place of HLT. To check out the operation of a program, leave a HLT in it temporarily, then when you're sure it operates correctly replace the HLT with a NOP for continuous running.

Chapter Ten

The Status Word and Flag Bits

PROCESSOR STATUS

In the previous section, you learned how to use the unconditional JMP instruction to tell the 8080 CPU to jump (or branch) to a specified memory address. The jump is one of the most valuable tools you will use in writing machine language programs.

But even more valuable are the *conditional* jump instructions, which tell the computer to jump to a different address *if and only if* a certain condition is met. Conditional jump instructions give the computer the ability to make decisions and perform alternate operations, based on the result of some previous test.

There are five conditions that the processor can test for. Three of these conditions will be introduced in this section. But first a little background:

A condition is the result of a test; you might say, "I'm going to the bank next Tuesday." Then each day you check the calendar to see if that day is Tuesday. When the calendar says that today is Tuesday, then the condition is met, and you perform the operation of going to the bank. Certain of the 8080 instructions are conditional—they specify that *IF* something happened, then the instruction is to be performed; if not, then the processor goes on to the next instruction.

In order to understand and use conditional jumps, you must first understand the status bits (or status flags) which are contained in the processor status word (PSW). The processor status word is located in register F. The status bits each indicate the result of a previous test. Each status bit is, of course, one bit—

therefore, a status bit can be a zero or a one. If the bit is a one, then we say that bit is *set* and the condition it represents is present, or has occurred. If a status bit is a zero, then we say that bit is *reset* or *clear* and the condition is not present, or did not occur.

The processor status word is the eight-bit byte, or contents, of register F. The status word actually contains only five status flags; the remaining three bits are not used. The table below illustrates the status word and the positions of the five status bits. In this text, we will discuss only three of the five flags, as follows:
 a. The SIGN flag, bit D_7.
 b. The ZERO flag, bit D_6.
 c. The CARRY flag, bit D_0.

The Processor Status Word—Register F

D_7	D_6	D_5	D_4	D_3	D_2	D_1	D_0
SIGN	ZERO	0	AUX CARRY	0	PARITY	1	CARRY

ZERO BIT

If an instruction produces 000Q (00000000B) in the accumulator, then the Zero bit will be set ($Z=1$). If any other value ends up in the accumulator, then the Zero bit will be reset ($Z=0$).

SIGN BIT

As you know by now, there are two hundred fifty-six different combinations of binary numbers from 00000000B to 11111111B; and they are sometimes used to represent the decimal numbers 0 to 255. However, sometimes the binary eight-bit byte is used to represent the decimal numbers from *minus* 128 to *plus* 127, thus allowing a standard byte to indicate a positive or negative number. Here's how it looks:

$$+ 127 \text{ decimal} = 01111111 \text{ binary}$$
$$+ 1 \text{ decimal} = 00000001 \text{ binary}$$
$$0 \text{ decimal} = 00000000 \text{ binary}$$
$$- 1 \text{ decimal} = 11111111 \text{ binary}$$
$$- 128 \text{ decimal} = 10000000 \text{ binary}$$

The Status Word and Flag Bits

As an example, if the accumulator contains 00000010B (decimal 2), and the SBI 005 (Subtract five) instruction is executed, then the result will be 11111101B (a negative three). Binary numbers always seem a little awkward at first. Just remember that if the leftmost bit is a *one*, then the number is considered negative.

Getting back to the Sign bit, if an operation such as addition, subtraction, ANDing, etc., results in a negative number the Sign bit will be set (S = 1). If a result is positive the Sign bit will be reset (S = 0).

To understand how certain instructions affect the processor status word flags you must be able to relate the digits on the front panel to the corresponding bits in the status word.

First, notice in the figure below, the locations of the Sign (S) and the Zero (Z) bits—none of the other status bits is shown yet:

The Processor Status Word

| S | Z | | | | | | |

From the figure above, you can see that the Sign and Zero bits of the processor status word occupy the leftmost two bits in register F. Notice that the leftmost two bits in the status word correspond to the leftmost digit in the front panel display. Here are some examples:

Case 1: The result of some previous instruction* is a byte in the range 001Q to 177Q (00000001B to 01111111B). That is a positive, non-zero byte so the Sign flag will not be set (S = 0) and the Zero flag will not be set (Z = 0).

| 0 | 0 | | | | | | |

0

Case 2: The result of a previous instruction is zero (00000000B). In this case the Sign bit will not be set (S = 0), and the Zero bit will be set (Z = 1).

| 0 | 1 | | | | | | |

1

---

* That is, the most recent instruction of a type that affects the Sign and Zero bits.

Case 3: The result of a previous instruction is a byte in the range 200Q to 377Q (10000000B to 11111111B). In this case, the Sign bit will be set (S=1), and the Zero bit will not be set (Z=0).

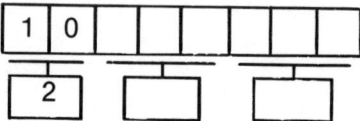

These three cases are the *only* possibilities. Case 4, in which the Sign bit and the Zero bit are both set is not possible. Why not? Read on!

A result cannot be *both* negative and zero. Therefore, the leftmost two bits in the status word can't both be set at the same time and the leftmost octal digit in register F can never be 3Q. Here's a summary:

SIGN BIT	ZERO BIT	LEFT OCTAL DIGIT IN REGISTER F
0	0	0
0	1	1
1	0	2
1	1	not possible

Note that if the result of a previous instruction is in the range 000Q to 177Q, the Sign bit will be zero (S=0). Bytes in this range can be interpreted as non-negative (zero or positive). Bytes in the range 200Q to 377Q can be interpreted as negative numbers, as discussed on page 86. For results in the negative range, the Sign bit will be set (S=1).

Exercise: Show how you would interpret the Sign and Zero flag bits if the following octal digits showed in the F register display:

REGISTER F	SIGN BIT	ZERO BIT
0 0 3	_____	_____
1 2 6	_____	_____
2 0 6	_____	_____
1 2 7	_____	_____
0 0 2	_____	_____

The Status Word and Flag Bits

CARRY BIT

Now look at the other end of the status word, at the rightmost bit where the Carry bit is located.

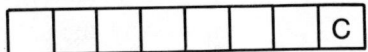

The Carry bit becomes set (C = 1) when the result of an operation is larger than 377Q. That is, the Carry bit is set when the result is too big to be contained in an eight-bit byte.

Since the Carry bit is the end bit, you can always tell whether it is set (C = 1) or not set (C = 0) by looking at the rightmost octal display digit for register F. If the digit is even, the Carry bit is 0; if the digit is odd, the Carry bit is 1.

It will take a little practice to learn how to interpret the PAM-8 display for register F, and then pick the Sign, Zero, and Carry bits out of it. The following series of short exercises will show you the effects of certain instructions on the Sign, Zero, and Carry flag bits. In addition, you'll get some practice in interpreting the status bits from your examination of the front panel display of register F.

In each of the following exercises, enter the program, run it, and then examine registers A and F after each HLT instruction. Record the octal values displayed in A and F in the blanks provided. Then fill in the blanks with a 0 or 1 to indicate the state of the Sign, Zero, and Carry bits. Notice that the middle octal digit in the F register is of no interest.

Exercise:

ADDRESS	CODE	INSTRUCTION	REG A	REG F	S	Z	C
040 100	227	SUB A					
040 101	166	HLT	___	___	___	___	___
040 100	227	SUB A					
040 101	166	HLT	___	___	___	___	___
040 102	306	ADI 001					
040 103	001						
040 104	166	HLT	___	___	___	___	___
040 100	227	SUB A					
040 101	166	HLT	___	___	___	___	___
040 102	306	ADI 200					
040 103	200						
040 104	166	HLT	___	___	___	___	___

After the second HLT, the status flag bit S has been set (S = 1), indicating that the result of executing the previous instruction was a value greater than 177Q.

Remember that when interpreting the Sign bit (0 = non-negative numbers, 1 = negative numbers) the octal numbers 001Q through 177Q are positive, and the octal numbers 200Q through 377Q are negative. You can also say that the numbers 000Q through 177Q are non-negative since for the case of zero (000Q) the Sign bit is not set (S = 0). You may wish to review page 86 for a more complete discussion of positive and negative numbers.

Exercise:

ADDRESS	CODE	INSTRUCTION	REG A	REG F	S	Z	C
040 100	076	MVI A,200					
040 101	200						
040 102	306	ADI 201					
040 103	201						
040 104	166	HLT	___	___	___	___	___
040 100	076	MVI A,200					
040 101	200						
040 102	306	ADI 200					
040 103	200						
040 104	166	HLT	___	___	___	___	___
040 100	076	MVI A,377					
040 101	377						
040 102	306	ADI 377					
040 103	377						
040 104	166	HLT	___	___	___	___	___

The status flags are affected when an instruction is executed — various instructions that you have already learned and used will affect the status flags. Some instructions *never* affect *any* of the five flag bits. Other instructions may affect one or more of the flags, depending on the result of the operation performed. Some instructions may affect all five flags.

The table below lists the machine instructions you have learned so far. For each instruction, the table shows which, if any, of the status flags are affected by the instruction.

The Status Word and Flag Bits

INSTRUCTION	STATUS FLAGS AFFECTED
LDA addr	none
STA addr	none
MVI R,data	none
MOV R_1,R_2	none
HLT	none
NOP	none
CALL addr	none
JMP addr	none
INR R	SIGN, ZERO
DCR R	SIGN, ZERO
ADI data	SIGN, ZERO, CARRY
SUI data	SIGN, ZERO, CARRY
ADD R	SIGN, ZERO, CARRY
SUB R	SIGN, ZERO, CARRY

SELF TEST

1. Fill in the octal op codes, enter the program, run it, and fill in the blanks at each HLT instruction. Set the display to registers AF.

ADDRESS	OP CODE (OCTAL)	MNEMONIC	REGISTERS A (IN OCTAL)	F	S	Z	C
040 100	_____	SUB A					
040 101	_____	HLT (#1)*	000	126	___	___	___
040 102	_____	ADI 001					
040 103	_____						
040 104	_____	HLT (#2)	___	___	___	___	___
040 105	_____	ADI 176					
040 106	_____						
040 107	_____	HLT (#3)	___	___	___	___	___
040 110	_____	ADI 001					
040 111	_____						
040 112	_____	HLT (#4)	___	___	___	___	___
040 113	_____	ADI 177					
040 114	_____						
040 115	_____	HLT (#5)	___	___	___	___	___

* The HLT instructions are numbered in reference to the next question in the test.

040 116	_____	ADI 001
040 117	_____	
040 120	_____	HLT (#6) ___ ___ ___ ___ ___
040 121	_____	ADI 100
040 122	_____	
040 123	_____	HLT (#7) ___ ___ ___ ___ ___
040 124	_____	ADI 301
040 125	_____	
040 126	_____	HLT (#8) ___ ___ ___ ___ ___
040 127	_____	ADI 376
040 130	_____	
040 131	_____	HLT (#9) ___ ___ ___ ___ ___
040 132	_____	ADI 377
040 133	_____	
040 134	_____	HLT (#10) ___ ___ ___ ___ ___
040 135	_____	JMP 040 100 (Note: include this section of
040 136	_____	the program to allow you to go
040 137	_____	back and check your answers.)

2. Copy the octal values you recorded at HLT's #1 to #10 for registers A and F in the first two columns. Then convert the octal values to their binary equivalent in the next two columns. Copy or fill in the status of flag bits S, Z and C at each HLT.

HLT #	REGISTER A F (OCTAL)	REGISTER A F (BINARY)	S	Z	C
1					
2					
3					
4					
5					
6					
7					
8					
9					
10					

3. Below are listed some combinations for status flags S, Z and CY. Fill in the blanks with HLT #1 to #10 to show where examples of these combinations occurred in the program. For combinations which could not occur, fill in the blank with the words "not possible."

The Status Word and Flag Bits

S	Z	CY	
0	0	0	_____
0	0	1	_____
0	1	0	_____
0	1	1	_____
1	0	0	_____
1	0	1	_____
1	1	0	_____
1	1	1	_____

Chapter Eleven

Conditional Jumps (JZ, JNZ, JC, JNC, JP, JM)

CONDITIONAL JUMPS

As noted in the previous section, the conditional jump instructions are very important. Like the unconditional jump instruction, the conditional jump instructions are each three bytes long, with bytes two and three containing the address of the location where the program is to branch. However, conditional jumps tell the computer to branch to an out-of-sequence location *only* if a certain condition is present.

The format for the conditional jump instructions is 3X2 octal. The middle octal digit is used to specify the condition as follows:

CODE	CONDITION	MIDDLE DIGIT
NZ	Not zero	0
Z	Zero	1
NC	No carry	2
C	Carry	3
PO	Parity odd*	4
PE	Parity even*	5
P	Positive sign	6
M	Minus sign	7

---

*Parity is generally an error checking method, and will not be discussed in this book.

As an example, Jump if not zero would be 302Q.

The op-codes for the eight conditional jump instructions are shown below:

OP-CODE	MNEMONIC	DESCRIPTION
302	JNZ	Jump if not zero
312	JZ	Jump if zero
322	JNC	Jump if no carry
332	JC	Jump if carry
342	JPO	Jump if parity is odd
352	JPE	Jump if parity is even
362	JP	Jump if positive
372	JM	Jump if minus

Each of these instructions would be followed by two bytes giving the address to be jumped to *if* the condition is met.

Another way of interpreting the conditional jump instructions is in terms of the corresponding status flags. The table below shows this for the six conditional jumps we'll be studying in this text:

OP-CODE	MNEMONIC	DESCRIPTION
302	JNZ	Jump if the zero flag is not set
312	JZ	Jump if the zero flag is set
322	JNC	Jump if the carry flag is not set
332	JC	Jump if the carry flag is set
362	JP	Jump if the sign flag is not set
372	JM	Jump if the sign flag is set

Important note: Remember that if a flag is set, it's a one. If a flag is not set, it's a zero.

To begin let's write some short programs using the Jump-if-not-zero and the Jump-if-zero instructions.

The first program directs the computer to count down from three (3) to zero (0), and then stop. The countdown will occur in the accumulator. The program can be broken down into three steps:

1. Place 3 into register A.
2. Decrement the count (in A) by one.
3. If the count in A is not zero, jump back to step 2, otherwise, HLT.

Conditional Jumps

A flow chart of the three steps would look like:

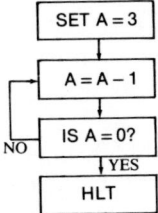

Here's the program:

ADDRESS	CODE	INSTRUCTION	COMMENT
040 100	076	MVI A,003	Put 003Q into the accumulator.
040 101	003		
040 102	075	DCR A	Decrement the accumulator.
040 103	302	JNZ 040 102	Jump if not zero to 040 102Q.
040 104	102		
040 105	040		
040 106	166	HLT	

Remember how the JNZ instruction works: Jump back if the zero flag is not set ($Z=0$). Don't jump back if the zero flag is set ($Z=1$).

The DCR instruction is the key to the whole program—it is the test that triggers the zero flag to be set or reset. If the DCR instruction causes the value in the accumulator to be zero, then the zero flag will be set ($Z=1$). Any time the value in the accumulator is not zero, then the zero flag is reset.

If you feel confused at this point, have faith, and take a look at the trace on the following page—we will take the program one step at a time and examine the zero flag at each step.

ADDRESS	INSTRUCTION	REG A	ZERO FLG	COMMENT
040 100	MVI A,003	003	X	Flag not affected.
040 102	DCR A	002	0	Zero flag *reset*.
040 103	JNZ 040 102	002	0	Jump occurs because Zero flag *not* set.
040 102	DCR A	001	0	Zero flag reset.
040 103	JNZ 040 102	001	0	Jump occurs because Zero flag not set.
040 102	DCR A	000	1	Zero flag *set*.
040 103	JNZ 040 102	000	1	Jump does not occur because Z flag is set.
040 106	HLT	000	1	End of program.

The logic involved here is a little confusing, but it's important — so read through each step, noting the relationship between the accumulator and the Zero flag. The Zero flag is set (Z = 1) only when the accumulator value becomes zero.

Exercise: Verify the trace by storing the program in memory, then single-step through it.
1. Single-step first with the display set to AF, then
2. Single step through with the display set to PC.
3. Can you see that if the instruction JZ (Jump if Zero) had been used at address 040 103Q, then the computer would have passed straight through and halted? JZ will jump back only when the Zero flag is set (Z = 1).

Instead of counting down in register A, the program can be made to count down in B, C, D, E, H, or L. The program below is similar to the previous one except:
1. The countdown occurs in register B, and
2. A HLT instruction is included in the loop so that you can see more easily the values in register B.

ADDRESS	CODE	INSTRUCTION	COMMENT
040 100	006	MVI B,003	Set the initial count to 3.
040 101	003		
040 102	166	HLT	Halt to observe register B.
040 103	005	DCR B	Decrease the count by one.
040 104	302	JNZ 040 102	If the count does not equal zero
040 105	102		jump back to 040 102Q.
040 106	040		
040 107	166	HLT	End of program.

Exercise: Store the program in memory, then run it with the display set to register B. Then run it with the display set to F. Finally run it with the display set to PC. Complete the table below, showing the register contents:

	RUN #1 Reg B	RUN #2 Reg F	RUN #3 PC
First HLT	___	___	___
Second HLT	___	___	___
Third HLT	___	___	___
Fourth HLT	___	___	___

Conditional Jumps

FIVE BEEPS

The next program directs the computer to count down from five to zero. Each time the count is reduced by one, the horn will beep. The JNZ instruction is used to repeat a loop until the count becomes zero. A flow chart of the program is below:

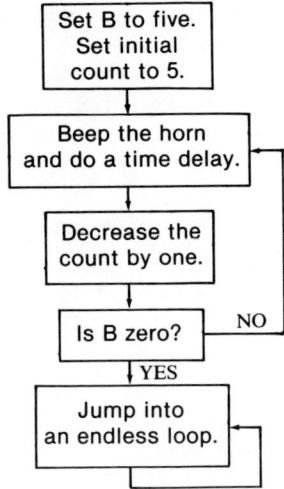

The *endless loop* at the end of the program is used instead of HLT, in order to prevent the extra BEEP which always occurs when a HLT is executed.

Here's the program:

ADDRESS	CODE	INSTRUCTION	COMMENT
040 100	006	MVI B,005	Put 005Q into register B.
040 101	005		
040 102	000	NOP	We'll use this space later.
040 103	000	NOP	
040 104	000	NOP	
040 105	000	NOP	
040 106	000	NOP	
040 107	000	NOP	
040 110	076	MVI A,377	Set the length of beep.
040 111	377		
040 112	315	CALL 002 140	Call the BEEP subroutine.
040 113	140		
040 114	002		

040 115	076	MVI A,377	Set the length of delay.
040 116	377		
040 117	315	CALL 000 053	Call the DELAY subroutine.
040 120	053		
040 121	000		
040 122	005	DCR B	Decrement the count.
040 123	302	JNZ 040 110	Go back to 040 110Q if the Z flag is not set. (Jump back if register B is not zero.)
040 124	110		
040 125	040		
040 126	303	JMP 040 126	This *jump-to-self* loop is just another way to stop the computer. This way there's no BEEP.
040 127	126		
040 130	040		

Note the last loop in the program. This is an endless loop. When the computer gets to address 040 125Q, it sees a JMP 040 125 — there's only one way to stop it: Hold the 0 and # keys down at the same time, and the program will stop.

Exercise:

1. Enter and run the program, with the display set to show the action in register B. Did it beep five times?
2. Change the count at 040 101Q to 003Q. Rerun the program. Did you get three beeps?
3. Now change the count at 040 101Q to 000Q. How many beeps this time? What do you think happened? The problem is at address 040 122Q — if there is initially a 000Q in register B, and you decrement it, then B will contain 377Q (00000000B minus one becomes 11111111B). And you'll really get your share of beeps with 377Q in B!

The third run points out a flaw in the program. To increase your sophistication as a programmer, take this as a warning — be sure to thoroughly test the programs you write. This is part of the debugging process. It's been said that any program of significant size will have bugs, but if you thoroughly test the programs after they're written, the number of bugs can be reduced and hopefully eliminated.

How could we correct the bug in our program? One way would be to jump out of the normal sequence of instructions if the value in register B is zero.

Conditional Jumps   101

COMPARE IMMEDIATE INSTRUCTION

The compare immediate (CPI) instruction is a two-byte instruction that compares one byte to the accumulator without changing the value in the accumulator. Again, it's one of the more useful 8080 instructions, and it comes in real handy if you ever want to test the accumulator to see if a particular data byte is there. The instruction format is:

    376   CPI XXX
    XXX

where the data byte XXX is the byte to be compared to the accumulator. The compare immediate instruction does affect the condition bits. If the two values are the same, the Zero bit will be set. Compare immediate actually subtracts the data byte from the accumulator, but it does *not* put the result back into the accumulator, as Subtract Immediate (SUI) does. With compare immediate, the accumulator remains unchanged.

JUMP IF ZERO

Jump if zero (JZ) is simple enough; if the Zero bit is set (if it is a *1*) then the jump will occur. It's just the opposite of JNZ.

Armed with these two new instructions, let's modify the previous program to fix the bug in it.

The new program:

ADDRESS	CODE	INSTRUCTION	COMMENT
040 100	006	MVI B,XXX	Put the initial count into B.
040 101	XXX		
040 102	170	MOV A,B	Move to A, the data in B.
040 103	376	CPI 000	Compare the data with 000Q.
040 104	000		
040 105	312	JZ 040 126	Jump if zero to 040 126Q.
040 106	126		
040 107	040		
040 110	076	MVI A,377	Set length of beep.
040 111	377		

040 112	315	CALL 002 140	Call the BEEP subroutine.
040 113	140		
040 114	002		
040 115	076	MVI A,377	Set length of delay.
040 116	377		
040 117	315	CALL 000 053	Call DELAY subroutine.
040 120	053		
040 121	000		
040 122	005	DCR B	Decrement the count.
040 123	302	JNZ 040 110	Jump back to 040 110Q if register B is not zero.
040 124	110		
040 125	040		
040 126	303	JMP 040 126	Self loop, when done.
040 127	126		
040 130	040		

The code from 040 103Q to 040 107Q fixes the program; for the case when the count is initially zero, there will be no beeps.

Look closely at the program and try to visualize what is happening. At 040 102Q the contents of register B (the count) is moved to the accumulator. At 040 103Q this value is compared to 000Q. If they are the same, the Zero flag bit will be set, and a Jump-if-zero will occur. Notice that any octal number could be put at 040 104Q; it does not have to be 000Q. If the octal number 030Q was put there, then when the count in register B reached 030Q (if ever) the Zero bit would be set and the Jump-if-zero would occur.

Exercise: Run the program with the "bug fix," as shown above. Try several values in register B by modifying address 040 101Q. Try zero. Does it work now?

Chapter Twelve

Input Subroutine, Guessing Game

KEYBOARD INPUT SUBROUTINE

Programmers never really "finish" a program. There is always some way to make the program work better, or make it perform the same task using fewer instructions. The counting program in Chapter Eleven would be much easier to use if the initial count could be input from the keyboard, instead of having to manually place it at address 040 101Q. Once again, the PAM-8 monitor comes to our rescue with the keyboard input subroutine—all you need to do is CALL it and it will return to the program with a number from the keyboard in the accumulator. The subroutine is located at address 003 260Q, and when this address is called, the computer will stay locked into that subroutine until a key is pressed. When a key is pressed, the computer will return to the main program. Let's take our counting program and modify it so that the initial count is taken from the keyboard.

ADDRESS	CODE	INSTRUCTION	COMMENT
040 100	315	CALL 003 260	Get a value from the PAM-8
040 101	260		keyboard.
040 102	003		
040 103	376	CPI 000	Is it 000Q?
040 104	000		
040 105	312	JZ 040 100	If the number is zero, no beeps are
040 106	100		performed. Jump back to get
040 107	040		another number.
040 110	107	MOV B,A	Move the number to register B.

040 111	076	MVI A,377	Set length of beep.
040 112	377		
040 113	315	CALL 002 140	Call BEEP subroutine.
040 114	140		
040 115	002		
040 116	076	MVI A,377	Set length of delay.
040 117	377		
040 120	315	CALL 000 053	Call DELAY subroutine.
040 121	053		
040 122	000		
040 123	005	DCR B	Decrement the count.
040 124	302	JNZ 040 111	Go back to 040 111Q if the count in
040 125	111		register B ≠ 0.
040 126	040		
040 127	303	JMP 040 100	After all beeps are completed, go
040 130	100		back to get another number.
040 131	040		

Here is a flow chart:

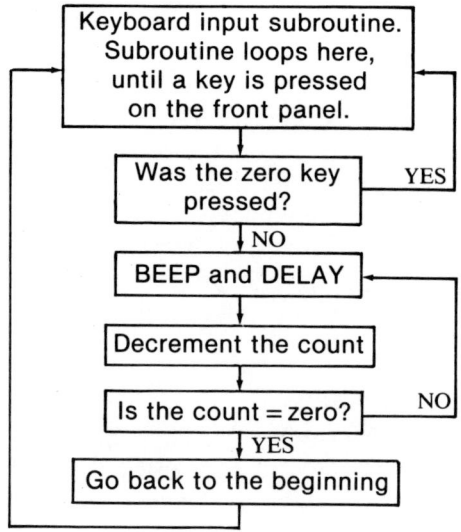

The addition of the input subroutine makes use of the program a lot easier. Now, a number is simply typed on the PAM-8 keyboard, and the corresponding number of beeps are heard.

Input Subroutine, Guessing Game

Exercise:
1. Enter the program and run it. Try each number 0 to 9, one at a time. Do they all give the correct number of beeps?
2. Try the + key. How many beeps? _____
3. Try the − key. How many beeps? _____
4. Try the * key. How many beeps? _____
5. Try the / key. How many beeps? _____
6. Try the # key. How many beeps? _____
7. Try the • key. How many beeps? _____

The input subroutine will make programming a lot easier, and, as you will see, every time you learn a new programming tool you can write more powerful programs.

GUESSING GAME

Now that you can input a number from the keyboard, all kinds of program variations are possible. The next program is a guessing game, which is merely a variation of our previous program. Here's how the game will work:
1. Player A will enter a secret number (0-9) on the keyboard. (Player B can't watch.)
2. Player B then enters his guess on the keyboard.
3. The computer will then subtract the two numbers. If they are the same, beeps will be heard. If they are different, the computer goes quietly back for another guess.

Here's the program:

Guessing Game

ADDRESS	CODE	INSTRUCTION	COMMENT
040 100	315	CALL 003 260	Call the INPUT subroutine. (Player
040 101	260		A enters a number.)
040 102	003		
040 103	107	MOV B,A	Move to B, the contents of reg A.
040 104	315	CALL 003 260	Call the INPUT subroutine. (Player
040 105	260		B guesses a number.)
040 106	003		
040 107	220	SUB B	Subtract B from A.
040 110	302	JNZ 040 104	If the two numbers are not the same,
040 111	104		jump back to 040 104 and input
040 112	040		another guess.

040 113	026	MVI D,003	Move 003Q to register D. (Register D is the BEEP counter.)
040 114	003		
040 115	076	MVI A,200	Set length of beep.
040 116	200		
040 117	315	CALL 002 140	Call BEEP subroutine.
040 120	140		
040 121	002		
040 122	076	MVI A,200	Set length of delay.
040 123	200		
040 124	315	CALL 000 053	Call DELAY subroutine.
040 125	053		
040 126	000		
040 127	025	DCR D	Decrement reg D (Beep counter).
040 130	302	JNZ 040 115	If the Beep counter ≠ 0 then jump back and BEEP some more.
040 131	115		
040 132	040		
040 133	303	JMP 040 100	Jump back to the beginning of the game.
040 134	100		
040 135	040		

The number 003Q at 040 114Q will give you three BEEPS if the guess is correct.

Exercise: Enter the program and run it. Type a number on the keyboard, then have someone else try to guess it by entering

their guess on the keyboard. If no BEEPS are heard the guess was wrong, so try another number. When player B finally guesses the number, the computer will beep three times. After that, the computer will automatically return to the beginning of the program and wait for another secret number from player A.

Chapter Thirteen

Random Number Generator, Output Subroutine

THE RANDOM NUMBER GENERATOR

One of the most interesting things about computers is that they're so precise. They never do anything on their own. Therefore, it's hard to make your computer *pick a number*. For years, programmers have been trying to write a program which would produce a string of non-repetitive numbers, *completely* at random. Many of these type programs have been written, and most of them produce numbers which seem random, and that's good enough to fool most people. The concept of random numbers is important. A subroutine that generates a string of non-predictable numbers is necessary for any program that causes the computer to pick a number, or deal an imaginary deck of cards, or roll a pair of imaginary dice. Such a subroutine is called a *random number generator*.

One simple way to get numbers at random from the computer is to have it count through a series of numbers (say 0 to 9) and stop the count at some random place. Remember that the computer is *very* fast, so as it counts there will be no way to predict where it will stop when we hit the stop key.

This next program will use register E to count 9 to 0 (9, 8, 7, 6, 5, 4, 3, 2, 1, 0, 9, 8, 7, 6, etc.). When the program is stopped, there will be a random number between 0 and 9 in register E.

Random Number Generator:

ADDRESS	CODE	INSTRUCTION	COMMENT
040 200	036	MVI E,011Q	Put 9 (decimal) into register E.
040 201	011		
040 202	035	DCR E	Count down to 1.
040 203	302	JNZ 040 202	Go back and count down again if the count ≠ 0.
040 204	202		
040 205	040		
040 206	303	JMP 040 200	When the count reaches 0, go back to 040 200Q and start counting again.
040 207	200		
040 210	040		

Exercise: Enter the program into memory and run it. After a few seconds, press the 0 and # keys. One of the numbers (0 to 9) should be in register E. Remember that 9 decimal is 011Q and 8 decimal is 010Q and so on.

Start and stop the program several times, each time checking register E to see what number is there.

With this new subroutine, you can go back to the number guessing program in chapter 12 and insert the random number generator for player A; the computer will then choose the first number and player B can try to guess it! Make these changes in the program:

ADDRESS	CODE	INSTRUCTION	COMMENT
040 100	303	JMP 040 200	Jump to the random number generator and get a number in register E.
040 102	200		
040 102	040		
040 103	103	MOV B,E	Move to B, the contents of register E.

That's all there is to it. Here is the new procedure for the game:
1. Set PC to 040 100Q.
2. Press 4 .
3. After a few seconds press 0   # .
4. Reset PC to 040 103Q.
5. Press 4 .
6. Enter your guesses until you get it right (BEEPs).
7. Go back to step 3.

Exercise: Modify the program to count how many guesses it took to find the correct answer.

Random Number Generator, Output Subroutine

Hints: Use an unused register to count up 1 after each guess. Stop the program when the guess is correct. Examine the register to see how many guesses it took.

USING FRONT PANEL DISPLAY

A program to display a message on the H8 front panel is shown on pages 1-23 of the Heathkit H8 Operators Manual. The program is rather complicated to explain in a few words. Therefore, we will use a simpler approach to display one digit of the display at a time.

Each digit on the display has a memory address which is used to refer to that particular digit. There are nine digits:

040 013 040 014 040 015   040 016 040 017 040 020   040 021 040 022 040 023

Each segment of each digit is assigned a particular bit of data as shown below. A zero in the assigned bit turns ON the segment, a one in the assigned bit turns OFF the segment. Here are the segment bit assignments:

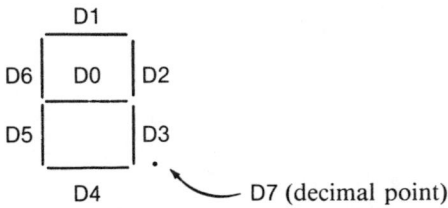

For example, to make a square in the upper portion of the digit, you'd turn on segments numbered D1, D2, D0, and D6. The *data byte* to be supplied to the program would be 10111000B, with zeros in the D1, D2, D0, and D6 positions. The digit would light up like this:

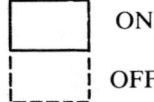

THE OUTPUT SUBROUTINE

Here's a program which will display one data byte on one of the digits of the 9-digit front panel display. The program is separated into its functional parts with comments provided to explain what each part does:

ADDRESS	CODE	INSTRUCTION	COMMENT
040 100	076	MVI A,002	When 002Q is stored at 040 010Q,
040 101	002		the PAM-8 monitor releases
040 102	062	STA 040 010	control of the front panel to the
040 103	010		user, and allows you to display
040 104	040		what you want to.
040 105	076	MVI A,ddd	You supply a data byte here to
040 106	ddd		display what you want to.
040 107	062	STA mmm nnn	This stores the data byte you want to
040 110	nnn		display into one of the nine front
040 111	mmm		panel display digits.
040 112	016	MVI C,020	This part of the program is merely a
040 113	020		time delay to hold the lights on
040 114	076	MVI A,377	long enough to be read. The data
040 115	377		byte at 040 113Q may be increased
040 116	315	CALL DELAY	to allow for a longer display time.
040 117	053		The data byte 020Q will give a
040 120	000		display of 9 or 10 seconds.
040 121	015	DCR C	
040 122	302	JNZ 040 114	
040 123	114		
040 124	040		
040 125	166	HLT	Stop. (The digit will go back to its original value.)

Remember:
1. ddd at address 040 106Q is the data byte to be displayed; a 270Q at that address would give a box display, as shown above.
2. mmm nnn at address 040 110Q and 040 111Q selects the digit which is to be lit.

Exercise:
1. Some typical light patterns with their data bytes are:

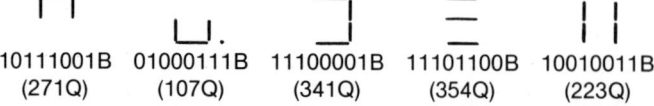

| 10111001B | 01000111B | 11100001B | 11101100B | 10010011B |
| (271Q) | (107Q) | (341Q) | (354Q) | (223Q) |

Try to duplicate the patterns by inserting the indicated octal data byte at address 040 106Q. Use display-digit address 040 013Q, which will be the leftmost digit of the front panel display. Try a few more patterns on your own.

Random Number Generator, Output Subroutine   113

2. Complete the chart below to show what data byte would be placed at address 040 106Q in order to produce the corresponding *decimal* digit on the display:

DECIMAL DIGIT	BINARY BYTE	OCTAL BYTE	DISPLAY LOOKS LIKE
0	10000001B	201Q	⎕
1	11110011B	363Q	⎜
2	11001000B	310Q	⊏
3	11100000B	340Q	⊒
4	10110010B	___	⊔
5	___	___	⊑
6	___	___	⊡
7	___	___	⌐
8	___	___	⊟
9	10110000B	260Q	⎕

SECTION THREE

Chapter Fourteen

Review

This final section will be your reward for sticking with it through the tedious exercises in sections one and two. Section Three will introduce a few more games, and you should be getting used to the PAM-8 monitor so that entering the longer programs is not as tiring.

Here is a summary of the instructions introduced so far:

NAME	CODE	INSTRUCTION
Load Accumulator	072	LDA mmm nnn
Store Accumulator	062	STA mmm nnn
Add Immediate	306	ADI ddd
Subtract Immediate	326	SUI ddd
Compare Immediate	376	CPI ddd
Move Immediate	0X6	MVI R,ddd
Move	1DS	MOV R_1,R_2
Add Register	20X	ADD R
Subtract Register	22X	SUB R
Increment Register	0X4	INR R
Decrement Register	0X5	DCR R
Jump	303	JMP mmm nnn
Jump if Zero	312	JZ mmm nnn
Jump if Not Zero	302	JNZ mmm nnn
Jump if Carry	332	JC mmm nnn
Jump if No Carry	322	JNC mmm nnn

Jump if Plus	362	JP mmm nnn
Jump if Minus	372	JM mmm nnn
Call	315	CALL mmm nnn
Return	311	RET
Halt	166	HLT
No Operation	000	NOP

Chapter Fifteen

Register Pairs
(LXI, INX, DCX, RRC, RLC)

REGISTER PAIRS

As you well know by now, in 8080 programming an address is 16 bits and a register is half that—8 bits. Sometimes registers are paired together to represent an address. The H and L registers are most often paired, and when they are, the term *register M* is used to refer to the data byte at that address. If register H contains 040Q and register L contains 200Q, then the register pair HL represents address 040 200Q. The instruction LXI H will load register pair HL with two data bytes—it's the same as MVI H and MVI L, except it can be done in one instruction.

The register pairs can be incremented (as a pair) using the INX instruction. The INX instruction considers the register pair to be a single, sixteen bit number, and increments it as such:

	H is L is (Octal)	Address HL is (Binary)
initially	000 375	00000000 11111101
after INX	000 376	00000000 11111110
another INX	000 377	00000000 11111111
another INX	001 000	00000001 00000000
another INX	001 001	00000001 00000001
another INX	001 002	00000001 00000010

There is also a Decrement Register Pair instruction (DCX) which takes a register pair as a single, sixteen bit number and decrements it. *Neither INX nor DCX will affect the flag bits the way INR and DCR do.*

Here's a program that will illustrate the use of register pair HL:

ADDRESS	CODE	INSTRUCTION	COMMENT
040 100	041	LXI H,040 200	Load H with 040Q and L with 200Q.
040 101	200		Register pair HL now refers to
040 102	040		address 040 200Q.
040 103	076	MVI A,100	Move 100Q into the accumulator.
040 104	100		
040 105	167	MOV M,A	Move the data byte in A to the address HL.
040 106	043	INX H	Increment address HL. ←——— NEW
040 107	074	INR A	Increment the accumulator.
040 110	376	CPI 110	Compare A with 110Q.
040 111	110		
040 112	302	JNZ 040 105	If not 110Q, then jump back to
040 113	105		address 040 105Q.
040 114	040		
040 115	166	HLT	

Remember that *M* refers to the *data* in memory at address HL. The program will store bytes 100Q through 110Q into ad-

Register Pairs

dresses 040 200Q through 040 210Q. In other words, the program will do this:

ADDRESS	DATA
040 200	100
040 201	101
040 202	102
040 203	103
040 204	104
040 205	105
040 206	106
040 207	107
040 210	110

Exercise: Enter the program and run it, then check the addresses 040 200Q through 040 210Q to see that the correct data was stored there.

How would you modify the program to make it store data bytes 000Q through 100Q into addresses 040 200Q through 040 300Q?

Other register pairs are used in the 8080 language:

INSTRUCTION	CODE
LXI H is	041Q
LXI D is	021Q
LXI B is	001Q

but *M* is *only* used to refer to the data at register pair HL.

ROTATE THE ACCUMULATOR

The data byte in the accumulator can be *rotated* in the following way: If the accumulator contains 00111111B, after rotating it one bit to the right it contains 10011111B. Notice that each bit moved one place to the right, *and* the least significant bit (the one on the right) moved around to the most significant position.

00111111

⌐10011111⌐

There is an 8080 op-code for rotating right (RRC), and there is also one for rotating left (RLC). For either instruction, if a *1* is rotated off the end of the byte, it will cause the Carry bit (in the flag word) to be set.

As an example, suppose we put 00000001B into the accumulator. Then rotate it left until the *1* bit rotates off the left end of the byte.

Here's the program:

ADDRESS	CODE	INSTRUCTION	COMMENT
040 100	076	MVI A,001	Put 00000001B into register A.
040 101	001		
040 102	000	NOP	These are for later.
040 103	000	NOP	
040 104	000	NOP	
040 105	007	RLC	Rotate the accumulator left.
040 106	322	JNC 040 104	Jump to 040 104Q if no CARRY occurred.
040 107	104		
040 110	040		
040 111	166	HLT	Stop.

Exercise:

1. Enter the program and run it. After it halts, examine the accumulator. What does it contain? Does this seem like the correct value?
2. The program should have looped eight times, rotating the bit from the far right position to the far left position and then back to the far right. Remember using a register as a counter back in Chapter Six? How would you use this technique to count the number of *rotates* in our program?

    Hint: Try using register B for counting—set it to zero initially with the MVI B,0 instruction, and then increment it each time there is a rotate.
3. Enter the new instructions into addresses 040 102Q to 040 104Q and run the program, then look at register B. Does it signify eight rotates?

MULTIPLY BY TEN

In our decimal number system it's easy to multiply a number by ten—just add a zero to the right of the least significant digit. For example a decimal 7 becomes a decimal 70. But how would you multiply the binary number 00000111B by ten? Adding a zero just doesn't work, but this will:

```
MOV A,B
RLC
RLC
ADD B
RLC
```

This short program will multiply the number in register B by ten and leave the answer in the accumulator. Let's try it with a binary seven:

ADDRESS	CODE	INSTRUCTION	COMMENT
040 100	006	MVI B,007	Put 007Q into register B.
040 101	007		
040 102	170	MOV A,B	Move into A, the contents of B.
040 103	007	RLC	
040 104	007	RLC	Multiply by ten and put the result
040 105	200	ADD B	into A.
040 106	007	RLC	
040 107	166	HLT	Stop.

Exercise: You guessed it — enter the program and run it. Then examine register A. What does it contain in binary? What does that translate to in decimal? Can you figure out how the routine works?

Exercise: There are many ways to multiply a number by ten in binary. Can you think of a different method? (Don't write a program, but try to think of another method.)

Chapter Sixteen

AND/OR Logic (ANI, ORI)

AND/OR LOGIC

AND/OR logic is a way of comparing bits. The rules are:

> 0 AND 0 is 0
> 0 AND 1 is 0
> 1 AND 0 is 1
> 1 AND 1 is 1
>
> 0 OR 0 is 0
> 0 OR 1 is 1
> 1 OR 0 is 1
> 1 OR 1 is 1

You will run across AND/OR logic very often in learning programming—it's a powerful tool for testing single bits, but it can also be used to test whole bytes:

if the accumulator contains	00000110
and if we AND it with	00000111
then the result is	00000110
now suppose the accumulator is	01101111
and we AND it with	00000111
this time the result is	00000111

Can you see that by ANDing the accumulator with 00000111B we are in effect *looking* at the last three bits in the accumulator?

The result always tells us exactly what the last three bits were. Many times in programming, you will want to look at a particular bit, or group of bits in the accumulator. The And Immediate instruction (ANI) will do just that; it's a two-byte instruction that ANDs the accumulator with a data byte, and leaves the result in the accumulator.

OR logic is similar but in programming it is commonly used to SET a bit, or group of bits — for instance:

if the accumulator contains	00000110
and if we OR it with	00110000
then the result is	00110110
now suppose the accumulator is	01101111
and we OR it with	00110000
then the result is	01111111

Notice that bits four and five are always a *1*. You will find that OR logic is a good way to make a bit, or group of bits be high. The instruction OR Immediate is a two-byte op-code that ORs the accumulator with a data byte, and leaves the result in the accumulator. OR Immediate is ORI.

EXCLUSIVE-OR

As shown above, when two bits are ORed the result will be a *1* if *either* or *both* bits are *1*. The rules for OR are:

BIT A	BIT B	A OR B
0	0	0
0	1	1
1	0	1
1	1	1

The results for Exclusive-OR are similar, except that *both* bits must be *different* to get a *1*. Exclusive-OR is shortened: XOR. The rules for XOR are:

BIT A	BIT B	A XOR B
0	0	0
0	1	1
1	0	1
1	1	0 ← Note

AND/OR Logic

Exercise:
1. AND the following bytes:

   | 00100101 | 11110000 | 10101010 | 00001111 | 11000011 |
   | 10001000 | 00001111 | 11111111 | 10101010 | 00000111 |

   | 00000000 | 11001010 | 01011111 | 11111111 | 01111111 |
   | 01110101 | 00110101 | 11111111 | 00000000 | 01100010 |

2. OR the following bytes:

   | 00100101 | 11110000 | 10101010 | 00001111 | 11000011 |
   | 10001000 | 00001111 | 11111111 | 10101010 | 00000111 |

   | 00000000 | 11001010 | 01011111 | 11111111 | 01111111 |
   | 01110101 | 00110101 | 11111111 | 00000000 | 01100010 |

3. If any byte is ANDed with 11111111B what will the result be?
4. If any byte is ORed with 11111111B what will the result be?
5. If any byte is ANDed with 00000000B what will the result be?
6. If any byte is ORed with 00000000B what will the result be?

Chapter Seventeen

More Random Numbers (XRA)

MORE RANDOM NUMBERS

The random number generator you studied in Chapter Thirteen was used to generate a number from one to nine. Remember the seven step procedure you had to go through to stop the random number generator, and then return to the program? That procedure was necessary because the action of stopping the program at some random place is what produced a random number.

The program described below will generate a random number all by itself, without you having to stop the program. In other words, you could CALL this program, and it will HALT with a random number in the accumulator.

ADDRESS	CODE	INSTRUCTION	COMMENT
041 000	041	LXI H,041 021	Load registers H and L with
041 001	021		041 021Q.
041 002	041		
041 003	176	MOV A,M	Move to register A, the contents of address HL.
041 004	017	RRC	Rotate the accumulator right one bit.
041 005	206	ADD M	Add the accumulator to M. (M is the data byte at address HL.)
041 006	017	RRC	Rotate the accumulator right.
041 007	167	MOV M,A	Move to M, the contents of A.
041 010	043	INX H	Increment the address HL.

041 011	256	XRA M		M is *exclusive-ORed* with the accumulator.
041 012	167	MOV M,A		Move to M, the contents of A.
041 013	000	NOP		
041 014	000	NOP		
041 015	166	HLT		Halt, to examine register A.
041 016	303	JMP 041 000		Jump back to 041 000Q and get another number.
041 017	000			
041 020	041			
041 021	022	ADDR1		These two locations are used to temporarily store data during the program
041 022	001	ADDR2		

The idea here is to designate two memory locations (ADDR1 and ADDR2) for temporary storage; take whatever data byte happens to be at ADDR1, change it slightly, then OR it with the data byte at ADDR2; and store the result back in ADDR2.

Exercise:
1. Assume address 041 021Q contains 022Q (00010010B) and address 041 022Q contains 001Q (00000001B). With a piece of scratch paper and a pencil, work through the program on paper and find out what number will be generated.
2. Load the program into memory, store 022Q at 041 021Q and store 001Q at 041 022Q. Then start at 041 000Q and run. What number is in the accumulator when the program halts? _____ Is that the correct result? _____
3. Continue running the program, and each time it halts, the data at address 041 021Q and 041 022Q will have changed. Since the number in the accumulator depends on the data at those two addresses, a different number will be in the accumulator each time.

Here is another version of the program with ANI 007 inserted just before the HLT, which will limit the number generated to the range 0-7:

Random Number Generator

ADDRESS	CODE	INSTRUCTION	COMMENT
041 000	041	LXI H,041 021	Load registers H and L with 041 021Q.
041 001	021		
041 002	041		

More Random Numbers

041 003	176	MOV A,M	Move to register A, the contents of address HL.
041 004	017	RRC	Rotate accumulator right one bit.
041 005	206	ADD M	Add the accumulator to M.
041 006	017	RRC	Rotate accumulator right one bit.
041 007	167	MOV M,A	Move to M, the contents of A.
041 010	043	INX H	Increment the address HL.
041 011	256	XRA M	M is *exclusive-ORed* with the accumulator.
041 012	167	MOV M,A	Move to M, the contents of A.
041 013	346	ANI 007	AND the accumulator with
041 014	007		00000111B.
041 015	166	HLT	Halt to observe the accumulator.
041 016	303	JMP 041 000	Jump back to generate another
041 017	000		number.
041 020	041		
041 021	XXX	ADDR1	
041 022	XXX	ADDR2	

By ANDing the accumulator with 00000111B, we will assure that the result in the accumulator is never greater than 00000111B (007Q).

For example, if at address 040 212Q in the program the accumulator contains 00101001B (decimal 41), after ANDing with 00000111B it is 00000001B (decimal 1). Remember that for most computational instructions such as ADD, SUB, AND, OR, and so on, *the result of the computation is left in the accumulator.*

How would you change the program to assure that the random number generated would never be larger than a decimal 15?

Chapter Eighteen

DICE

With all that you've learned up to now, you can write some very interesting programs. How about letting the computer generate two random numbers at a time, in the range of decimal 1 to decimal 6—in effect the computer would become a set of electronic dice! The logic involved is simple enough:

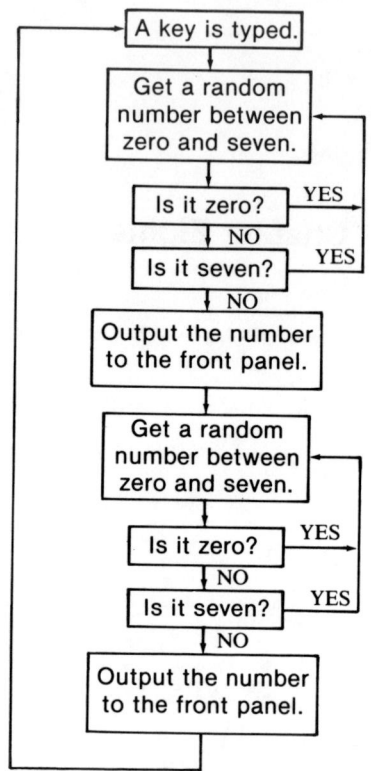

Here's the DICE program:

ADDRESS	CODE	INSTRUCTION	COMMENT
040 100	315	CALL 003 260	Call the input subroutine.
040 101	260		
040 102	003		
040 103	315	CALL 041 000	Call the random number generator.
040 104	000		
040 105	041		
040 106	346	ANI 007	AND the accumulator with
040 107	007		00000111B.
040 110	312	JZ 040 103	If the number in the accumulator is
040 111	103		zero, jump back to 040 103Q.
040 112	040		
040 113	376	CPI 007	Compare the accumulator with 007Q.
040 114	007		

DICE

040 115	312	JZ 040 103	If the number in the accumulator is
040 116	103		seven, jump back to 040 103Q.
040 117	040		
040 120	315	CALL 040 300	Call Output subroutine #1.
040 121	300		
040 122	040		
040 123	315	CALL 041 000	Call the random number generator.
040 124	000		
040 125	041		
040 126	346	ANI 007	AND the accumulator with
040 127	007		00000111B.
040 130	312	JZ 040 123	If the number in the accumulator is
040 131	123		zero, jump back to 040 123Q.
040 132	040		
040 133	376	CPI 007	Compare the accumulator with 007Q.
040 134	007		
040 135	312	JZ 040 123	If the number in the accumulator is
040 136	123		seven, jump back to 040 123Q.
040 137	040		
040 140	315	CALL 040 330	Call Output subroutine #2.
040 141	330		
040 142	040		
040 143	303	JMP 040 100	Jump back for another roll of the
040 144	100		dice.
040 145	040		

The same random number generator shown in Chapter Thirteen will work fine for this program, providing a RETURN instruction is added at the end. After a number is generated, you want control transferred back to the main program.

The program is repeated here for your convenience:

Random Number Generator

ADDRESS	CODE	INSTRUCTION	COMMENT
041 000	041	LXI H,041 021	Load registers H and L with
041 001	021		041 021Q.
041 002	041		
041 003	176	MOV A,M	Move to A, the contents of M.
041 004	017	RRC	Rotate accumulator right.
041 005	206	ADD M	Add the accumulator to M.

041 006	017	RRC	Rotate accumulator right.
041 007	167	MOV M,A	Move to M, the contents of A.
041 010	043	INX H	Increment the address HL.
041 011	256	XRA M	Exclusive-OR register M with A.
041 012	167	MOV M,A	Move to M, the contents of A.
041 013	311	RET	Return to the main program.
041 014	000	NOP	
041 015	000	NOP	
041 016	000	NOP	
041 017	000	NOP	
041 020	000	NOP	
041 021	022	ADDR1	
041 022	001	ADDR2	

Notice that the ANI instruction was removed at 041 013Q; it could have been left in, but is not needed because the main program contains ANI 007.

Two output subroutines are necessary because the roll of the dice is to be displayed in the two rightmost digits of the PAM-8 front panel display. A different subroutine is needed for each digit since the rightmost display digit is addressed 040 023Q, and the next digit over is addressed 040 022Q. Here are the routines:

ADDRESS	CODE	INSTRUCTION	COMMENT
040 300	107	MOV B,A	Move to B, the contents of A.
040 301	076	MVI A,002	This allows us access to the PAM-8
040 302	002		front panel.
040 303	062	STA 040 010	
040 304	010		
040 305	040		
040 306	170	MOV A,B	Move to A, the contents of B.
040 307	062	STA 040 023	Store at 040 023Q (display digit).
040 310	023		
040 311	040		
040 312	016	MVI C,020	This is a time delay to keep the digit
040 313	020		lit long enough to see it.
040 314	076	MVI A,377	
040 315	377		
040 315	315	CALL 000 053	
040 317	053		
040 320	000		

DICE

040 321	015	DCR C	
040 322	302	JNZ 040 314	
040 323	314		
040 324	040		
040 325	311	RET	Return to main program.

The above will be Output subroutine #1. Here's Output subroutine #2:

ADDRESS	CODE	INSTRUCTION	COMMENT
040 330	107	MOV B,A	Move to B, the contents of A.
040 331	076	MVI A,002	This allows us access to the PAM-8
040 332	002		front panel.
040 333	062	STA 040 010	
040 334	010		
040 335	040		
040 336			
040 336	170	MOV A,B	Move to A, the contents of B.
040 337	062	STA 040 022	Store at 040 022Q (display digit).
040 340	022		
040 341	040		
040 342	016	MVI C,020	This is a time delay to keep the digit
040 343	020		lit long enough to see it.
040 344	076	MVI A,377	
040 345	377		
040 346	315	CALL 000 053	
040 347	053		
040 350	000		
040 351	015	DCR C	
040 352	302	JNZ 040 344	
040 353	344		
040 354	040		
040 355	311	RET	Return to the main program.

Compare the entire program to the logic blocks at the beginning of this chapter and notice how the program is broken down into sections (or blocks) — each section is performing a precise task. This is an important idea. In later programming on your own, you'll be following three main steps to write a program:

1. Decide what the program should accomplish.
2. Design the program logic blocks.
3. Write the actual programming instructions.

Exercise:
1. Load the program into memory; the whole program must be in memory or it will not work, so verify that the main program, the random number generator, and both output routines are loaded into memory properly. Run the program. With the program running, the right two digits of the display should display numbers from one to six whenever any key is typed on the keyboard.
2. How would you modify the program to simulate the roll of five dice? All you Yahtzee players can have electronic dice, too!

Chapter Nineteen

HI-LO, General Purpose Output Routine

HI-LO

This next program is a game similar to the number guessing game studied in Chapter Twelve, except that the computer gives you clues in this one. The computer picks a number at random, and you try to guess it—if your guess is too high, the display says *HI*—if your guess is too low, the display says *LO*—and if you get the number correct, the display flashes and beeps. Below is a logic diagram describing the program:

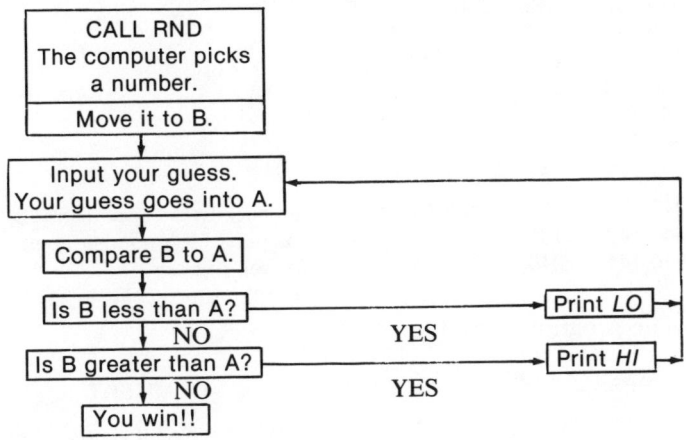

Here's the program:

HI-LO

ADDRESS	CODE	INSTRUCTION	COMMENT
040 100	315	CALL 041 000	Call the random number generator.
040 101	000		
040 102	041		
040 103	107	MOV B,A	Move to B, the contents of A.
040 104	315	CALL 003 260	Call the INPUT subroutine. (Inputs a number from the PAM-8 front panel into register A.)
040 105	260		
040 106	003		
040 107	270	CMP B	Register B is compared to A.
040 110	372	JM 040 150	If the result is minus, jump to 040 150Q.
040 111	150		
040 112	040		
040 113	362	JP 040 165	If the result is positive, jump to 040 165Q.
040 114	165		
040 115	040		
040 116	026	MVI D,005	This is the *win* section: this subroutine causes the display to flash and the audio to beep, five times. Register D is used to count five cycles. No particular character is sent to OUT1 and OUT2, but when they are CALLed, the digits momentarily flash.
040 117	005		
040 120	076	MVI A,377	
040 121	377		
040 122	315	CALL 002 140	
040 123	140	(BEEP)	
040 124	002		
040 125	315	CALL 040 330	
040 126	330	(OUT2)	
040 127	040		
040 130	315	CALL 040 300	
040 131	300	(OUT1)	
040 132	040		
040 133	025	DCR D	
040 134	302	JNZ 040 120	
040 135	120		
040 136	040		
040 137	303	JMP 040 100	Jump back to the beginning. The computer picks another number for you to guess.
040 140	100		
040 141	040		

The program continues:

ADDRESS	CODE	INSTRUCTION	COMMENT
040 150	076	MVI A,217	This subroutine outputs *LO* to the display.
040 151	217	(L)	
040 152	315	CALL 040 330	

HI-LO, General Purpose Output Routine

040 153	330	(OUT2)	
040 154	040		
040 155	076	MVI A,201	
040 156	201	(O)	
040 157	315	CALL 040 300	
040 160	300	(OUT1)	
040 161	040		
040 162	311	RET	Return to the main program.
040 163	000	NOP	
040 164	000	NOP	
040 165	076	MVI A,222	This subroutine outputs *HI* to the
040 166	222	(H)	display.
040 167	315	CALL 040 330	
040 170	330	(OUT2)	
040 171	040		
040 172	076	MVI A,363	
040 173	363	(I)	
040 174	315	CALL 040 300	
040 175	300	(OUT1)	
040 176	040		
040 177	311	RET	Return to the main program.

The digits HI and LO were formed as shown in Chapter Thirteen:

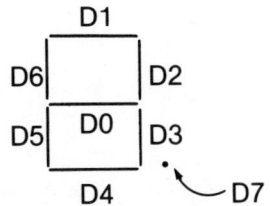

H is 10010010B (222Q)
I is 11110011B (333Q)
L is 10001111B (217Q)
O is 10000001B (201Q)

Use exactly the same random number generator as you used in the previous program. The random number generator should be located starting at 041 000Q and must be in memory for the program to work.

Look again at the flow chart at the beginning of the chapter. Compare it to the program carefully and make sure you understand the logic involved.

Why do you think the random number generated at the beginning of the program (the computer's guess) is immediately moved to register B?

Why do you think register D was used as the counter in the *win* subroutine?

A GENERAL OUTPUT ROUTINE

Our method for outputting data to the front panel so far has been to write a different output routine for each digit in the display. Since the recent programs have been using the rightmost two digits, we've had to write only two output subroutines. For programs using the whole display (nine digits), nine output routines would have to be written. So, how about *one* general purpose output subroutine, where we would specify which digit is to be used before the output subroutine is called. Such a routine is shown below; the digit to be used for display is put into H and L and the byte to be displayed is placed in the accumulator before the subroutine is called.

ADDRESS	CODE	INSTRUCTION	COMMENT
041 100	107	MOV B,A	Move to B, the contents of A. (The data byte to be displayed is originally in A, now it's in B.)
041 101	076	MVI A,002	Storing 002Q at 040 010Q tells the PAM-8 monitor to give us control of the front panel.
041 102	002		
041 103	062	STA 040 010	
041 104	010		
041 105	040		
041 106	160	MOV M,B	Move to address HL (M), the contents of register B. Address HL is the address of one of the front panel display digits.
041 107	016	MVI C,020	This is a delay loop which delays the display long enough for you to see it. The subroutine DELAY is not long enough by itself, so it's CALLed several times.
041 110	020		
041 111	076	MVI A,377	
041 112	377		
041 113	315	CALL 000 053	
041 114	053		
041 115	000		
041 116	015	DCR C	
041 117	302	JNZ 041 111	
041 120	111		
041 121	041		
041 122	311	RET	Return.

Chapter Twenty

Stars

In the game of Stars, the computer selects a random number from 1 to 100. You try to guess the number and the computer gives you clues to tell you how close you're getting. One star means your guess is far away from the number; seven stars means you're very close. You get seven guesses to find the secret number.

At first, this game might seem similar to HI-LO but the strategy is entirely different. The computer does not tell you if your guess is above or below the secret number — only how close it is.

The program uses the same random number generator located at 041 000Q to generate a secret number. The number is then tested to make sure it's not over 100 decimal. The heart of the program is testing the secret random number against the player's guess.

Let's look at some sample data bytes, and assume them to all be less than 01100100B (100 decimal).

The first example will be 00000001B (1 decimal). That data byte will have to be rotated left eight times in order to set the Carry bit. Therefore, if a data byte is assumed to be less than 100 decimal, and that data byte must be rotated left eight times before the Carry bit is set, then that data byte must be 1 or 0 decimal.

Now look at data byte 00000011B (3 decimal). That one will set the Carry bit when rotated left seven times. So, if a data byte must be rotated left seven times before the Carry bit is set, then that data byte must be 3 decimal or less.

Now consider the byte 00000111B (7 decimal). That one will set the Carry bit when rotated left six times. If a data byte must be rotated left six times in order to set Carry, then that data byte must be 7 decimal or less.

And so on.... You can see that the data byte 01100100B (100 decimal) would only have to be rotated twice in order to set the Carry bit.

The logic used in the Stars program is:
1. Get the computer's secret number (a random number between 1 and 100 decimal).
2. Input a guess from the player.
3. Determine which of the two numbers is larger and subtract the small number from the large one.
4. Then take the *difference* and use the *rotate left* method to award stars acording to how big the difference is—a large difference gets only a few stars, a small difference means the guess is very close, so a lot of stars are awarded.

Remember that the player is only allowed seven chances to guess the secret number.

Here's the program:

Stars

ADDRESS	CODE	INSTRUCTION	COMMENT
040 100	036	MVI E, 010	Set the *turn counter* initially. (The
040 101	010		player has 7 tries to win.)
040 102	315	CALL 041 000	Call the random number generator,
040 103	000		get a random number between zero
040 104	041		and one hundred and save it in
040 105	346	ANI 177	register D.

Stars

Here's a flow chart describing the program:

STARS

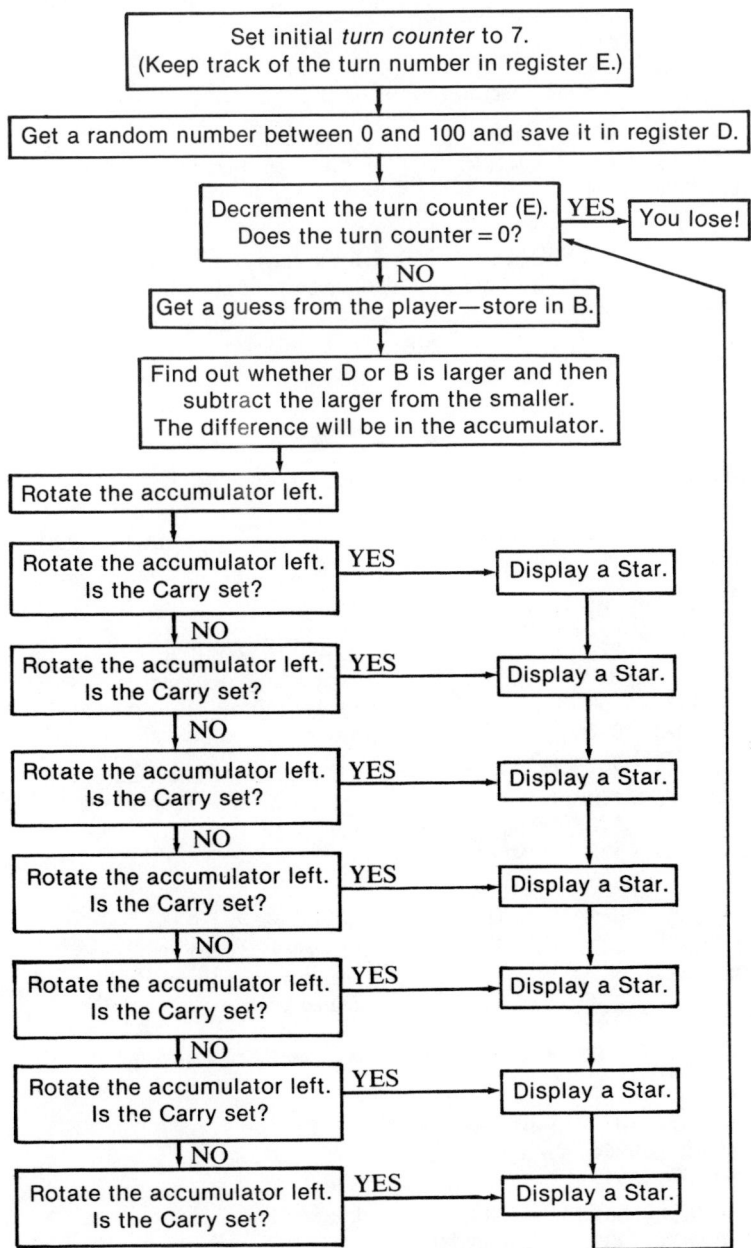

040 106	177		
040 107	376	CPI 144	
040 110	144		
040 111	362	JP 040 102	
040 112	102		
040 113	040		
040 114	127	MOV D,A	
040 115	035	DCR E	Decrement the *turn counter* (E) and
040 116	312	JZ 040 300	if it is zero then the player loses.
040 117	300		
040 120	040		
040 121	315	CALL 003 260	Get the player's guess (a two-digit
040 122	260	(Input)	number) and store in register B.
040 123	003		
040 124	107	MOV B,A	
040 125	007	RLC	
040 126	007	RLC	
040 127	200	ADD B	
040 130	007	RLC	
040 131	107	MOV B,A	
040 132	315	CALL 003 260	
040 133	260	(Input)	
040 134	003		
040 135	200	ADD B	
040 136	107	MOV B,A	
040 137	222	SUB D	Compare the player's input with
040 140	312	JZ 040 330	number in D (the computer's secret
040 141	330		number); if they're the same the
040 142	040		player wins.
040 143	362	JP 040 150	If the result of the above test is a
040 144	150		negative number, subtract the
040 145	040		other way.
040 146	172	MOV A,D	
040 147	220	SUB B	
040 150	007	RLC	This is the *rotate left* test. The
040 151	007	RLC	*difference* between the player's
040 152	332	JC 040 254	guess and the computer's number is
040 153	254		rotated left one bit at a time.
040 154	040		When the Carry gets set we know
			how big the difference is.
040 155	007	RLC	
040 156	332	JC 040 246	
040 157	246		
040 160	040		
040 161	007	RLC	
040 162	332	JC 040 240	

Stars

040 163	240		
040 164	040		
040 165	007	RLC	
040 166	332	JC 040 232	
040 167	232		
040 170	040		
040 171	007	RLC	
040 172	332	JC 040 224	
040 173	224		
040 174	040		
040 175	007	RLC	
040 176	332	JC 040 216	
040 177	216		
040 200	040		
040 201	007	RLC	
040 202	332	JC 040 210	
040 203	210		
040 204	040		
040 205	303	JMP 040 115	Go back for another guess.
040 206	115		
040 207	040		
040 210	041	LXI H,040 015	Print star #7.
040 211	015		
040 212	040		
040 213	315	CALL 041 076	
040 214	076	(Output)	
040 215	041		
040 216	041	LXI H,040 016	Print star #6.
040 217	016		
040 220	040		
040 221	315	CALL 041 076	
040 222	076	(Output)	
040 223	041		
040 224	041	LXI H,040 017	Print star #5.
040 225	017		
040 226	040		
040 227	315	CALL 041 076	
040 230	076	(Output)	
040 231	041		
040 232	041	LXI H,040 020	Print star #4.
040 233	020		
040 234	040		
040 235	315	CALL 041 076	
040 236	076	(Output)	
040 237	041		

040 240	041	LXI H,040 021	Print star #3.
040 241	021		
040 242	040		
040 243	315	CALL 041 076	
040 244	076	(Output)	
040 245	041		
040 246	041	LXI H,040 022	Print star #2.
040 247	022		
040 250	040		
040 251	315	CALL 041 076	
040 252	076	(Output)	
040 253	041		
040 254	041	LXI H,040 023	Print star #1.
040 255	023		
040 256	040		
040 257	315	CALL 041 076	
040 260	076	(Output)	
040 261	041		
040 262	303	JMP 040 115	Go back for another guess.
040 263	115		
040 264	040		
040 300	006	MVI B,003	This is the *you lose* section. It will
040 301	003		BEEP three times, and then stop.
040 302	076	MVI A,377	
040 303	377		
040 304	315	CALL 002 140	
040 305	140	(BEEP)	
040 306	002		
040 307	076	MVI A,377	
040 310	377		
040 311	315	CALL 000 053	
040 312	053	(Delay)	
040 313	000		
040 314	005	DCR B	
040 315	302	JNZ 040 302	
040 316	302		
040 317	040		
040 320	303	JMP 040 320	
040 321	320		
040 322	040		
040 324	000	NOP	
040 325	000	NOP	
040 326	000	NOP	
040 327	000	NOP	
040 330	006	MVI B,007	This is the *you win* section. It will
040 331	007		BEEP seven times, and then stop.
040 332	076	MVI A,100	

Stars

040 333	100	
040 334	315	CALL 002 140
040 335	140	(BEEP)
040 336	002	
040 337	076	MVI A,100
040 340	100	
040 341	315	CALL 000 053
040 342	053	(Delay)
040 343	000	
040 344	005	DCR B
040 345	302	JNZ 040 332
040 346	332	
040 347	040	
040 350	303	JMP 040 350
040 351	350	
040 352	040	

Since the PAM-8 front panel display will not display a star, the pattern ⌷ was chosen to represent a star. The data byte 10111000B (270Q) is put into the accumulator and then output to the proper digit on the display. The general purpose output subroutine shown at the end of Chapter Nineteen can be used, except that MVI A,270 must be put in front of it:

ADDRESS	CODE	INSTRUCTION	COMMENT
041 076	076	MVI A,270	Put a *star* into the accumulator.
041 077	270		
041 100	107	MOV B,A	
041 101	076	MVI A,002	
041 102	002		
041 103	062	STA 040 010	
041 104	010		
041 105	040		
041 106	160	MOV M,B	Output the data byte in register A to
041 107	016		the display digit specified by the
041 107	016	MVI C,020	address HL.
041 110	020		
041 111	076	MVI A,377	
041 112	377		
041 113	315	CALL 000 053	
041 114	053		
041 115	000		
041 116	015	DCR C	
041 117	302	JNZ 041 111	
041 120	000		
041 121	041		
041 122	311	RET	

If you understand how the program should work, enter it into memory and try running it. This is a long program, so don't try entering all that tedious code if you're tired or don't feel like concentrating. Enter the op-codes carefully, since one mistake will often prevent the program from running properly.

Once it's in the computer, you'll find the game of Stars to be a lot of fun.

YOU'RE ON YOUR OWN

At this point you've come a long way, and have a good understanding of 8080 machine language. The majority of the 8080 instructions have been covered in this book, and will provide a good foundation for your further study or experimentation.

With this knowledge you should now try to write your own program. Follow the pattern you've learned:
1. Decide what you want the computer to do.
2. Make a block diagram.
3. Write the code.
4. Enter and run the program.

Very often when you run the program for the first time it won't work—don't get discouraged, it's a fact of life for even the most experienced programmers. Review the program carefully and trace its operation one step at a time. If you can't find the mistake and a friend is available who's studying with you, ask him to follow it through. It's sometimes helpful to simply put the program away and come back to it later; a fresh approach at a later time can sometimes work wonders.

The 8080 instruction set is the set used for many of today's modern micro-computers. The Heath H8, Altair 8800, Imsai 8080, Polymorphics 8813, Processor Technology Sol, and many others are all based on the 8080. The 8080 instruction set is also the foundation for a whole other set of Central Processors including the 8085, 8086, and the Z-80. Machine language is tedious, but it's also very rewarding—and you'll vastly appreciate the higher level languages after knowing machine language.

The computer is a powerful tool, one limited only by the imagination of the user. Machine language is a difficult and involved subject to learn, and there aren't many texts of this sort written for the layman. We, the authors, sincerely hope you've found this book a help in understanding the fundamental 8080 language.

SECTION FOUR

Appendix I

The 8080 Op-Codes in Review

This section contains the instruction set one at a time, with a brief definition for each op-code. This will be a reference for you to consult in your later programming. The following applies for this section:

mmm,nnn   is defined as a 16 bit address whose two octal halves are mmm and nnn. For instance: for the address 040 100, mmm would be 040 and nnn would be 100.

ddd   is an octal data byte. The smallest octal data byte is 000Q, and the largest is 377Q.

X   is an octal digit in the range 0 through 7.

r   refers to one of the registers: A, B, C, D, E, H, or L.

000   **NOP — No operation**
Nothing happens. This instruction is used to fill space in a program. The computer sees the NOP, then goes on to the next instruction. Status bits not affected.

IN – Input

333
ddd
An eight bit byte is moved from the terminal device *ddd* into the accumulator. Status bits not affected.

OUT – Output

323
ddd
An eight bit byte is moved from the accumulator out to terminal device *ddd*. Status bits not affected.

JMP – Jump

303
nnn
mmm
The address mmm,nnn is put in the program counter. The computer will jump to address mmm,nnn. Status bits are not affected.

JNZ – Jump if not zero

302
nnn
mmm
If the Zero bit is 0 (the result of a previous test was not *zero*) then the computer will jump to address mmm,nnn; otherwise, operation continues with the next op-code.

JZ – Jump if zero

312
nnn
mmm
If the Zero bit is 1 (the result of a previous test *was* zero) then the computer will jump to address mmm,nnn; otherwise, operation continues with the next op-code.

JNC – Jump if no carry

322
nnn
mmm
If the Carry bit is 0 then no Carry has occurred and the computer will jump to address mmm,nnn; otherwise, operation continues with the next op-code.

JC – Jump if carry

332
nnn
mmm
If the Carry bit is 1 then a Carry has not occurred and the computer will jump to address mmm,nnn; otherwise, operation continues with the next op-code.

JP – Jump if positive

362
nnn
mmm
If the Sign bit is 0 (a *positive* result from a previous test) then the computer jumps to address mmm, nnn; otherwise, operation continues with the next op-code.

The 8080 Op-Codes in Review

372 nnn mmm	**JM — Jump if minus** If the Sign bit is 1 (a *negative* result from a previous test) then the computer jumps to address mmm, nnn; otherwise, operation continues with the next op-code.

The CALL instructions are similar to the JMP instructions except that when a CALL op-code is used, you usually intend to return back to the main program by use of the Return op-code. Before a CALL instruction is executed, the next sequential op-code address is stored on the Stack so that later when the Return instruction is encountered, the CPU will know what address to return to.

315 nnn mmm	**CALL — Call** The computer unconditionally moves to address mmm,nnn and executes the subroutine at that address.
304 nnn mmm	**CNZ — Call if not zero** If the Zero bit is 0 (the result of a previous test was *not* zero) then the computer moves operation to address mmm,nnn.
314 nnn mmm	**CZ — Call if zero** If the Zero bit is 1 (the result of a previous test *was* zero) then the computer moves operation to address mmm,nnn.
324 nnn mmm	**CNC — Call if no carry** If the Carry bit is 0 (a previous test resulted in *no* Carry) then the computer moves operation to address mmm,nnn.
334 nnn mmm	**CC — Call if carry** If the Carry bit is 1 (a previous test resulted in a Carry) then the computer moves operation to address mmm,nnn.
364 nnn mmm	**CP — Call if positive** If a previous test resulted in a positive number, then the Sign bit will be 0 and the CALL to address mmm,nnn will be made.

374 nnn mmm	**CM — Call if minus** If a previous test resulted in a negative number, then the Sign bit will be 1 and the CALL to address mmm,nnn will be made.

The RETURN instructions are used to return to the main program. When a CALL instruction is executed, the address of the next sequential op-code is automatically pushed onto the Stack. The subroutine CALLed will usually have a RETURN instruction in it. This instruction pops the address saved off of the Stack and operation resumes at that address. RETURNS may or may not be based on the Status word.

311	**RET-Return** The return address is popped off of the Stack and placed in the Program Counter. Operation then resumes at that address.
300	**RNZ — Return if not zero** If the Zero bit is 0 (a non-zero answer to a previous test) then the Return is executed.
310	**RZ — Return if zero** If the Zero bit is 1 (a zero answer to a previous test) then the Return is executed.
320	**RNC — Return if no carry** If the Carry bit is 0, then the Return will be made.
330	**RC — Return if carry** If the Carry bit is 1, then the Return will be made.
360	**RP — Return if positive** If the Sign bit is 0, then the Return will be made.
370	**RM — Return if minus** If the Sign bit is 1, then the Return will be made.

More than one Return can be used in a subroutine, and the instruction does not necessarily have to be at the end.

The 8080 Op-Codes in Review

THE ACCUMULATOR INSTRUCTIONS

007
RLC — Rotate the accumulator left
The accumulator byte is moved one bit to the left. Bit 7 wraps around into bit 0.

017
RRC — Rotate the acumulator right
The accumulator byte is moved one bit to the right. Bit 0 wraps around into bit 7.

027
RAL — Rotate accumulator left through carry
The accumulator byte is moved one bit to the left through the Carry bit. Example:
  accumulator = 00 000 111   and Carry = 0
then after RAL:
  accumulator = 00 001 110   and Carry = 0

037
RAR — Rotate the accumulator right through carry
The accumulator byte is moved one bit to the right through Carry. Example:
  accumulator = 00 000 111   and Carry = 0
then after RAR:
  accumulator = 00 000 011   and Carry = 1

057
CMA — Complement the accumulator
Each bit in the accumulator is complemented, which means that each *1* becomes a *0*, and each *0* becomes a *1*.

306
ddd
ADI — Add immediate to the accumulator
The data byte *ddd* is added to the accumulator and the result is put back into the accumulator. Status bits affected are Sign, Zero, and Carry.

326
ddd
SUI — Subtract immediate from the accumulator
The data byte *ddd* is subtracted from the accumulator and the result is put back into the accumulator. Status bits affected are Sign, Zero, and Carry.

346
ddd
ANI — AND immediate with the accumulator
The data byte *ddd* is ANDed with the accumulator and the result is put into the accumulator. Status

bits affected are Sign and Zero; the Carry bit is reset to 0.

ORI — OR immediate with the accumulator

366
ddd

The data byte *ddd* is ORed with the accumulator and the result is put into the accumulator. Status bits affected are Sign and Zero; the Carry bit is reset to 0.

XRI — Exclusive-OR immediate with the accumulator

356
ddd

The data byte *ddd* is Exclusive-ORed with the accumulator and the result is put into the accumulator. Status bits affected are Sign and Zero; the Carry bit is reset to 0.

CPI — Compare immediate to the accumulator

376
ddd

The data byte *ddd* is compared with the accumulator by subtracting it from the accumulator. The result is *not* put back into the accumulator — it remains unchanged. Status bits affected are Sign, Zero, and Carry.

STA — Store the accumulator

062
nnn
mmm

The contents of the accumulator are stored at address mmm,nnn. Status bits are not affected.

LDA — Load the accumulator

072
nnn

The data byte at address mmm,nnn is loaded into the accumulator. Status bits are not affected.

STC — Set carry

067

The Carry bit is set to 1. No other status bits are affected.

CMC — Complement the carry

077

The Carry bit is complemented; which means if it was zero, it's changed to one, and if it was one, then it's changed to zero. No other status bits are affected.

The 8080 Op-Codes in Review

The Increment, Decrement, Register, and Move instructions all use the following codes to denote the individual 8080 registers:

        Register B is 0
        Register C is 1
        Register D is 2
        Register E is 3
        Register H is 4
        Register L is 5
        Register M is 6 (M is the data at address HL)
        Register A is 7

INR — Increment register

0X4   The register specified by the octal digit X is incremented by one. The Sign and Zero bits are affected.

DCR — Decrement register

0X5   The register specified by the octal digit X is decremented by one. Sign and Zero bits affected.

MVI — Move immediate

0X6
ddd   The data byte *ddd* is moved into the specified register (or memory address HL). No Status bits are affected.

MOV — Move data

1DS   There are two variables in this instruction, D and S. D is the octal digit representing the destination register, and S is the octal digit representing the source register. When the MOV instruction is executed, data is moved from the source register to the destination register. After the instruction, both registers contain the same data byte. No status bits are affected.

REGISTER INSTRUCTIONS

ADD — Add register

20X   The specified register is added to the accumulator and the result is put into the accumulator. Sign, Zero, and Carry are affected.

22X
SUB — Subtract register
The specified register is subtracted from the accumulator and the result is put into the accumulator. Sign, Zero, and Carry are affected.

24X
ANA — AND register
The specified register is ANDed with the accumulator and the result is put into the accumulator. The Sign and Zero bits are affected. The Carry bit is reset to 0.

26X
ORA — OR register
The specified register is ORed with the accumulator and the result is put into the accumulator. The Sign and Zero bits are affected. The Carry bit is reset to 0.

25X
XRA — Exclusive-OR register
The specified register is Exclusive-ORed with the accumulator and the result is put back into the accumulator. Sign and Zero bits are affected. The Carry bit is reset to 0.

27X
CMP — Compare register
The specified register is compared with the accumulator by subtracting it from the accumulator. The result is *not* put back into the accumulator — it remains the same. The Sign, Zero, and Carry bits are affected.

PUSH, POP, AND LOAD

These three instructions have several variations depending on which register *pairs* are used. The codes for the register pairs are:

> Register pair B,C is 0
> Register pair D,E is 2
> Register pair H,L is 4
> The Stack pointer is 6
> Accumulator and Flag bits are also 6

The 8080 Op-Codes in Review

You can see that these codes follow along with the individual register codes as shown above.

LXI — Load register pair immediate

0X1
nnn
mmm

Two bytes of data are loaded into the specified register pair. The data *nnn* is loaded into the second register of the pair, and data *mmm* is loaded into the first register of the pair. Data mmm and nnn does not need to represent an address — although many times it does.

The Stack is a portion of memory where data or addresses are stored. Usually the Stack area is defined by the PAM-8 monitor, but the Stack can be set by the programmer using the LXI SP instruction shown above. The PUSH instruction moves the data contained in a register pair (two bytes) on to the Stack. *Two bytes* of data are always put on the Stack at a time. The POP instruction moves the top two bytes of data off the Stack and into the specified register pair. Two bytes of data are always removed from the Stack at a time.

PUSH — Push data onto the Stack

3X5

The contents of the specified register pair are stored in two bytes of memory, at an address pointed to by the Stack Pointer.

The contents of the first register are PUSHed into an address *one less than the Stack Pointer*; the contents of the second register are PUSHed into an address *two less than the Stack Pointer*.

POP — Pop data off of the Stack

3X1

The top two bytes of data on the Stack (defined by the Stack Pointer plus one, and the Stack Pointer plus two) are moved into the two registers specified by X.

INCREMENT/DECREMENT REGISTER PAIRS

As you've no doubt noticed, registers are often paired in 8080 programming. Thus a register pair can be used to represent a single 16 bit number. The INX (Increment) and DCX (Decrement) instructions consider the register pairs B,C; D,E; and

H,L as single 16 bit binary numbers. (The instructions only refer to the first register of the pair.) Therefore, if register B contains 00000000 and C contains 11111111B, then after the INX B opcode register B will contain 00000001B and register C will contain 00000000B. In other words 00000000B 11111111B was incremented to 00000001B 00000000B. The status bits are *not* affected. The op-codes are:

003	INX B — Increment register pair B,C.
023	INX D — Increment register pair D,E.
043	INX H — Increment register pair H,L.
063	INX SP — Increment the STACK pointer (which is a 16 bit number).
013	DCX B — Decrement register pair B,C.
033	DCX D — Decrement register pair D,E.
053	DCX H — Decrement register pair H,L.
073	DCX SP — Decrement the STACK pointer.

THE H,L OP-CODES

XCHG — Exchange registers

353   The 16 bit number in the H and L registers is exchanged with the 16 bit number in the D and E registers. In other words, H and D are exchanged, and L and E are exchanged. The Status bits are not affected.

XTHL — Exchange Stack

343   The data byte in register L is exchanged with the data at the Stack Pointer address, and the byte in register H is exchanged with the byte at the Stack Pointer address plus one. The Status bits are not affected.

SPHL — Load Stack Pointer from H,L

371   The 16 bit number represented by H,L replaces the Stack pointer; this moves the Stack. The H and L registers are unchanged. The Status bits are not affected.

The 8080 Op-Codes in Review

PCHL — Load Program Counter from H,L

351 This is in effect a jump instruction. The computer will jump to the address specified by the H and L registers and continue executing the program from there. H and L are not changed. The Status bits are not affected.

SHLD — Store H and L direct

042 The data byte in L is stored at address mmm,nnn;
nnn and the data byte in register H is stored at address
mmm mmm,nnn = 1. The Status bits are not affected.

LHLD — Load H and L direct

052 Register L is loaded with the data byte at address
nnn mmm,nnn; and register H is loaded with the data
mmm byte at address mmm,nnn = 1. The Status bits are not affected.

Appendix II

The Hexadecimal System

A hexadecimal digit is a shorthand way of representing four bits—the Hex digits are defined as:

HEX	DECIMAL	BINARY
0	0	0000
1	1	0001
2	2	0010
3	3	0011
4	4	0100
5	5	0101
6	6	0110
7	7	0111
8	8	1000
9	9	1001
A	10	1010
B	11	1011
C	12	1100
D	13	1101
E	14	1110
F	15	1111

Notice that since there are eight bits of information in a normal data byte, two hex digits will represent one byte. For instance, the binary data byte 00101010 would be 2A hex. That works out a little nicer than octal shorthand, where it takes three octal digits to represent one byte:

00101010 (Binary = 2A (Hex) = 052 (Octal)

But, since the octal system uses only the digits 0 through 7, and the hex system uses the digits 0 through 9 plus the letters A through F, we feel that the newcomer to computers is much more comfortable with octal. Also, the 8080 instruction set was designed with octal in mind. For these reasons this text was written using the octal shorthand system. You should remember that it's the *binary word* that's important, not which shorthand system is used to represent that word.

Appendix III

Sample Program

SUM OF INTEGERS 0-10

Program to add the numbers from 0 to 10 and store at 000 100.

ADDRESS	OP-CODE		EXPLANATION
000 000	006	MVI B,012	Move into register B the binary number
000 001	012		ten.
000 002	076	MVI A,000	Move into the accumulator the binary
000 003	000		number zero.
000 004	200	ADD B	Add register B to the accumulator (the result goes into the accumulator).
000 005	005	DCR B	Decrement register B.
000 006	302	JNZ 000 004	Jump if not zero back to address
000 007	004		000 004Q.
000 010	000		
000 011	062	STA 000 100	Store accumulator (sum of 0 through 10)
000 012	100		at address 000 100Q.
000 013	000		
000 014	303	JMP 000 014	Loop here when done.
000 015	014		
000 016	000		

This program puts a binary ten in register B and a zero in the accumulator, then adds them and the result goes back in the accumulator. The accumulator contains $0 + 10 = 10$. Then register B is decremented to 9 and added to accumulator. The accumulator contains $10 + 9 = 19$. Then register B is decremented to 8 and added to the accumulator, and so on. After register B becomes zero, the accumulator is stored at 000 100. It will be the binary number 00110111 (55).

Appendix IV

A Better Random Number Generator

The random number generator we've been using is okay for simple programs, but here's a much better generator.

ADDRESS	OP-CODE		EXPLANATION
000 000	041	LXI H,000 050	This generator uses four addresses for
000 001	050		temporary storage. They are
000 002	000		000 045Q, 000 046Q, 000 047Q, and
000 003	006	MVI B,010	000 050Q.
000 004	010		
000 005	176	MOV A,M	
000 006	007	RLC	
000 007	007	RLC	
000 010	007	RLC	
000 011	256	XRA M	
000 012	027	RAL	
000 013	027	RAL	
000 014	055	DCR L	
000 015	055	DCR L	
000 016	055	DCR L	
000 017	176	MOV A,M	
000 020	027	RAL	
000 021	167	MOV M,A	
000 022	054	INR L	
000 023	176	MOV A,M	
000 024	027	RAL	
000 025	167	MOV M,A	
000 026	054	INR L	
000 027	176	MOV A,M	
000 030	027	RAL	
000 031	167	MOV M,A	
000 032	054	INR L	
000 033	176	MOV A,M	

000 034	027	RAL
000 035	167	MOV M,A
000 036	005	DCR B
000 037	302	JNZ 000 006
000 040	006	
000 041	000	
000 042	XXX	Jump back to program or return.
000 043	XXX	
000 044	XXX	

Appendix V

ASCII Codes

BINARY	OCTAL	CHARACTER
00000000	000	NUL
00000111	007	BEL
00001010	012	line feed
00001101	015	carriage return
00100000	040	space
00100001	041	!
00100010	042	"
00100011	043	#
00100100	044	$
00100101	045	%
00100110	046	&
00100111	047	'
00101000	050	(
00101001	051	)
00101010	052	*
00101011	053	+
00101100	054	,
00101101	055	−
00101110	056	.
00101111	057	/
00110000	060	0
00110001	061	1
00110010	062	2
00110011	063	3
00110100	064	4
00110101	065	5
00110110	066	6

00110111	067	7
00111000	070	8
00111001	071	9
00111010	072	:
00111011	073	;
00111100	074	<
00111101	075	=
00111110	076	>
00111111	077	?
01000000	100	@
01000001	101	A
01000010	102	B
01000011	103	C
01000100	104	D
01000101	105	E
01000110	106	F
01000111	107	G
01001000	110	H
01001001	111	I
01001010	112	J
01001011	113	K
01001100	114	L
01001101	115	M
01001110	116	N
01001111	117	O
01010000	120	P
01010001	121	Q
01010010	122	R
01010011	123	S
01010100	124	T
01010101	125	U
01010110	126	V
01010111	127	W
01011000	130	X
01011001	131	Y
01011010	132	Z
01011011	133	[
01011100	134	\
01011101	135	]
01011110	136	∧
01011111	137	_

There are more ASCII codes, but these are the most common ones.

Appendix VI

Answers to Questions

Page 6

```
BINARY       SPLIT        OCTAL
11010001 = 11 010 001 =    321
10000100 = 10 000 100 =    204
00100001 = 00 100 001 =    041
11010011 = 11 010 011 =    323
00111000 = 00 111 000 =    070
11000111 = 11 000 111 =    307
```

```
OCTAL      SPLIT         BINARY
 303   = 11 000 011 = 11000011
 377   = 11 111 111 = 11111111
 042   = 00 100 010 = 00100010
 311   = 11 001 001 = 11001001
 257   = 10 101 111 = 10101111
 176   = 01 111 110 = 01111110
```

Page 8

```
16 bit binary:        1110110011010001
two bytes:        11 101 100   11 010 001
octal:               3 5 4       3 2 1
```

```
16 bit binary:        0011111001010011
two bytes:        00 111 110   01 010 011
octal:               0 7 6       1 2 3
```

```
16 bit binary:      1111100011111111
two bytes:       11 111 000   11 111 111
octal:              3 7 0       3 7 7
```

Page 9

```
040 100 = 00 100 000     01 000 000 = 00100000 01000000
077 377 = 00 111 111     11 111 111 = 00111111 11111111
041 245 = 00 100 001     10 100 101 = 00100001 10100101
036 260 = 00 011 110     10 110 000 = 00011110 10110000
```

Page 10

1. In this course we will frequently represent one byte, or eight bits, by an octal code consisting of *three* octal digits.

2. a. Q_0 can be 0, 1, 2, 3, 4, 5, 6 or 7.
    b. Q_1 can be **0, 1, 2, 3, 4, 5, 6 or 7**.
    c. Q_2 can only be **0, 1, 2 or 3**.

3. a. 00000001B = **001Q**.
    b. 00001000B = **010Q**.
    c. 01000000B = **100Q**.
    d. 01001001B = **111Q**.
    e. 10011100B = **234Q**.
    f. 01111111B = **177Q**.

4. a. 007Q = **00000111B**.
    b. 123Q = **01010011B**.
    c. 411Q = **not possible**.
    d. 377Q = **11111111B**.
    e. 600Q = **not possible**.

5. a. 0000000100000000B = **0 0 1   0 0 0Q**.
    b. 0000000011100101B = **0 0 0   3 4 5Q**.
    c. 0101001111010001B = **1 2 3   3 2 1Q**.
    d. 1111111100000000B = **3 7 7   0 0 0Q**.

6. a. 111 222Q = **01001001 10010010B**.
    b. 040 106Q = **00100000 01000110B**.
    c. 076 123Q = **00111110 01010011B**.
    d. 262 300Q = **10110010 11000000B**.

Answers to Questions

7. a. 377 377Q = **OK**.
    b. 077 077Q = **OK**.
    c. 123 321Q = **OK**.
    d. 244 444Q = **NO**.
    e. 077 777Q = **NO**.
    f. 045 306Q = **OK**.
    g. 543 000Q = **NO**.

8. 047 373 = 00100111 11111011
    047 374 = 00100111 11111100
    047 375 = **00100111 11111101**
    047 376 = **00100111 11111110**
    047 377 = **00100111 11111111**
    050 000 = **00101000 00000000**
    050 001 = **00101000 00000001**

9. The largest number using eight bits that can be written **in binary is 11111111** and **in octal is 377**.

Page 20

When an invalid memory address is examined (a location where there is no memory), the contents of that location will normally show 377 octal (11111111B). It's not a random value — it's always 377 octal.

Page 23

1. The key to use for examining the contents of a memory location is **#** .

2. When depositing a number in the memory location being shown on the display, use the **/** key.

3. A decimal point in every digit indicates that the PAM-8 monitor is ready to access a memory location.

4. A running decimal point in the display indicates that PAM-8 is ready to accept a change in the value stored at the memory location now being shown.

5. DO THIS   DISPLAY READS
   a. Press #   XXX XXX XXX
   b. Enter 040 234   **040 234** XXX
   c. Press /   **040 234** XXX
                                (with running decimal)
   d. Enter 333   **040 235** XXX
   e. Press −   **040 234 333**

6. Press # key,
   Enter 043 102,
   Press / key,
   Enter 200,
   Enter 201.

Page 33

Trace Chart

ADDRESS	CONTENTS OF ACCUMULATOR	CONTENTS OF MEMORY LOCATION			
		040 200	040 201	040 202	040 203
040 100	**111**				
040 102	111	**111**			
040 105	**222**	111			
040 107	222	111	**222**		
040 112	**111**	111	222		
040 115	111	111	222	**111**	
040 120	111	111	222	111	**111**
040 123	**333**	111	222	111	111
040 125	333	111	222	111	111

Page 39

STEP	ADDRESS	CODE	INSTRUCTION
1	040 100	**076**	MVI A,111
	040 101	111	
2	040 102	**306**	ADI 022
	040 103	022	
3	040 104	**062**	STA 040 200
	040 105	200	
	040 106	040	
4	040 107	**306**	ADI 135
	040 110	135	
5	040 111	**062**	STA 040 201
	040 112	201	
	040 113	040	

6	040 114	**072**	LDA 040 200
	040 115	200	
	040 116	040	
7	040 117	**166**	HLT
8	040 120	**072**	LDA 040 201
	040 121	201	
	040 122	040	
9	040 123	**166**	HLT

First HLt   133Q ⟵ Sum of first two numbers.
Second HLT 270Q ⟵ Final result.

Page 40

1. The accumulator is an example of **a register.**

2. A computer program is placed in memory in **sequential order.**

3. The STA instruction is a **3-byte instruction.**

4. The starting address in memory where a program is stored is usually the same (040 100Q), but does not have to always be the same.

5. As a debugging tool, many computers can step through a program one instruction at a time using the **single-step** operation.

6. The LDA instruction uses three bytes. Byte two contains the **LOW-order** address, and byte three contains the **HI-order** address.

7. Mnemonic op-codes are used as shorthand for binary instructions because **they are easier to remember.**

8. A breakpoint is a temporary stopping place in a program, placed there so that the flow of the program can be followed more easily.

9. The Program counter is a sixteen bit register located in the CPU which keeps track of the location of the next instruction to be executed.

10. After the program halts,
    a. The accumulator will contain **202Q**.
    b. Address 040 150Q will contain **101Q**.
    c. The Program will contain **040 111Q**.
    d. Address 040 111Q contains **202Q**.
    e. The contents of address 040 150Q **did change**.
    f. The contents of address 040 111Q **did not change**.
    g. The program occupies **ten** memory addresses.

11. | INSTRUCTION NAME | MNEMONIC | OCTAL OP-CODE |
    |---|---|---|
    | Move immediate | MVI A | 076 |
    | Add immediate | ADI | 306 |
    | Store accumulator | STA | 062 |
    | Load accumulator | LDA | 072 |
    | Halt | HLT | 166 |

12. MVI **Immediate mode**
    ADI **Immediate mode**
    STA **Direct mode**
    LDA **Direct mode**

13. Both **MVI A** and **ADI** are two-byte instructions.

14. **STA** and **LDA** are three-byte instructions, and must be followed by an address.

15. The STA instruction stores the contents of the accumulator into the specified memory address — **it does not change the contents of the accumulator.** In this case, the accumulator would still contain 111Q.

Page 44

STEP	ADDRESS	CODE	INSTRUCTION
1	040 100	**006**	MVI B,000
	040 101	000	
2	040 102	**016**	MVI C,011
	040 103	011	
3	040 104	**026**	MVI D,022
	040 105	022	

Answers to Questions

4	040 106	**036**	MVI E,033
	040 107	033	
5	040 110	**046**	MVI H,044
	040 111	044	
6	040 112	**056**	MVI L,055
	040 113	055	
7	040 114	**076**	MVI A,077
	040 115	077	
8	040 116	166	HLT

Page 46

1. MOV H,L   **1 4 5**

2. MOV L,H   **1 5 4**

3. MOV E,B   **1 3 0**

4. MVI L,111   **0 5 6   1 1 1**

5. MOV C,A   **1 1 7**

6. MVI C,377   **0 1 6   3 7 7**

7. MOV A,B   **1 7 0**

Page 48

Program to perform register *roll down*:

ADDRESS	CODE	INSTRUCTION	COMMENT
040 100	006	MVI B,001	Put 001Q into register B.
040 101	001		
040 102	016	MVI C,002	Put 002Q into register C.
040 103	002		
040 104	026	MVI D,003	Put 003Q into register D.
040 105	003		
040 106	036	MVI E,004	Put 004Q into register E.
040 107	004		
040 110	166	HLT	Halt.
040 111	173	MOV A,E	Move to A, the contents of E.

040 112	132	MOV E,D	Move to E, the contents of D.
040 113	121	MOV D,C	Move to D, the contents of C.
040 114	110	MOV C,B	Move to C, the contents of B.
040 115	107	MOV B,A	Move to B, the contents of A.
040 116	166	HLT	Halt.

Page 50

The MOVes must be done in the order:

    Move B to A,
    Move C to B,
    Move D to C,
    Move E to D.

This moves the value in each register up to the next register. The value in A is lost, and the value in registers E and D will be the same. If the MOVes were done in the order:

    Move E to D,
    Move D to C,
    Move C to B,
    Move B to A,

then after the MOVes, each register would contain the same value—the value in E.

Page 56

1. The MVI instruction will move a data byte into a specified register.

2. REGISTER   OCTAL DIGIT

    A = 7
    B = 0
    C = 1
    D = 2
    E = 3
    H = 4
    L = 5

3. The MOV instruction will move the contents of one register to another register.

4. When the ADD instruction is executed, the sum is placed in the accumulator.

5. The SUB instruction also places the result in the accumulator.

6. The INR instruction (Increment register) will add *1* to the specified register.

7. The DCR instruction (Decrement register) will subtract *1* from the specified register.

8. If register B contains 003Q and DCR B is executed four times the result in B will be 377Q:

INSTRUCTION	REGISTER B CONTAINS
MVI B,003	003
DCR B	002
DCR B	001
DCR B	000
DCR B	377

Page 70

ADDRESS	CODE	INSTRUCTION	COMMENT
040 100	076	MVI A,100	Program to begin counting at 100Q
040 101	100		and count upwards by ones.
040 102	074	INR A	
040 103	166	HLT	
040 104	303	JMP 040 102	
040 105	102		
040 106	040		

ADDRESS	CODE	INSTRUCTION	COMMENT
040 100	072	LDA 040 200	Program to begin counting with the
040 101	200		value stored at 040 200Q and count
040 102	040		upwards by ones.
040 103	074	INR A	
040 104	166	HLT	

040 105	303	JMP 040 103	
040 106	103		
040 107	040		
040 100	076	MVI A,100	Program to begin counting at 100Q
040 101	100		and count down by ones.
040 102	075	DCR A	
040 103	166	HLT	
040 104	303	JMP 040 102	
040 105	102		
040 106	040		

040 100	072	LDA 040 200	Program to begin counting with the
040 101	200		value stored at 040 200Q and count
040 102	040		down by ones.
040 103	075	DCR A	
040 104	166	HLT	
040 105	303	JMP 040 103	
040 106	103		
040 107	040		

Page 72

040 100	016	MVI C,000	Program to count upwards in register
040 101	000		C.
040 102	014	INR C	
040 103	166	HLT	
040 104	303	JMP 040 102	
040 105	102		
040 106	040		

Page 73

040 100	026	MVI D,000	This program counts upwards by
040 101	000		ones in registers D and E.
040 102	036	MVI E,000	
040 103	000		
040 104	024	INR D	
040 105	034	INR E	
040 106	166	HLT	
040 107	303	JMP 040 104	
040 110	104		
040 111	040		

Answers to Questions

040 100	046	MVI H,000	Program to count up in register H by ones, and down in register L by ones.
040 101	000		
040 102	056	MVI L,000	
040 103	000		
040 104	044	INR H	
040 105	055	DCR L	
040 106	166	HLT	
040 107	303	JMP 040 104	
040 110	104		
040 111	040		

Page 74

040 100	006	MVI B,000	Program to count upwards by twos in register B, starting at 000Q.
040 101	000		
040 102	004	INR B	
040 103	166	HLT	
040 104	303	JMP 040 102	
040 105	102		
040 106	040		

040 100	016	MVI C,000	Program to count upwards by twos in register C, starting at 000Q.
040 101	000		
040 102	014	INR C	
040 103	014	INR C	
040 104	166	HLT	
040 105	303	JMP 040 102	
040 106	102		
040 107	040		

040 100	016	MVI C,377	Program to count down by twos in register C, starting at 377Q.
040 101	377		
040 102	015	DCR C	
040 103	015	DCR C	
040 104	166	HLT	
040 105	303	JMP 040 102	
040 106	102		
040 107	040		

Page 75

040 100	026	MVI D,001	Program to count upwards by twos in register D, starting at 001Q. (Generates positive odd integers.)
040 101	001		
040 102	024	INR D	
040 103	024	INR D	
040 104	166	HLT	
040 105	303	JMP 040 102	
040 106	102		
040 107	040		

Page 76

040 100	026	MVI D,000	Program to generate partial sums of odd integers. Register E generates odd integers (1, 3, 5,...); register D holds the sums (1, 1+3, 1+3+5, 1+3+5+7,...).
040 100	000		
040 102	036	MVI E,001	
040 103	001		
040 104	172	MOV A,D	
040 105	203	ADD E	
040 106	127	MOV D,A	
040 107	166	HLT	
040 110	034	INR E	
040 111	034	INR E	
040 112	303	JMP 040 104	
040 113	104		
040 114	040		

Page 83

b. Increment register B:

ADDRESS	CODE	INSTRUCTION
040 100	227	SUB A
040 101	107	MOV B,A
040 102	117	MOV C,A
040 103	076	MVI A,XXX
040 104	XXX	

040 105	315	CALL 000 053
040 106	053	
040 107	000	
040 110	004	INR B
040 111	000	NOP
040 112	303	JMP 040 103
040 113	103	
040 114	040	

c. Increment register B *and* C:

040 100	227	SUB A
040 101	107	MOV B,A
040 102	117	MOV C,A
040 103	076	MVI A,XXX
040 104	XXX	
040 105	315	CALL 000 053
040 106	053	
040 107	000	
040 110	004	INR B
040 111	014	INR C
040 112	303	JMP 040 103
040 113	103	
040 114	040	

d. Count up by twos in register C:

040 100	227	SUB A
040 101	107	MOV B,A
040 102	117	MOV C,A
040 103	076	MVI A,XXX
040 104	XXX	
040 105	315	CALL 000 053
040 106	053	
040 107	000	
040 110	014	INR C
040 111	014	INR C
040 112	303	JMP 040 103
040 113	103	
040 114	040	

e. Count up in register C, *and* down in register B:

040 100	227	SUB A
040 101	107	MOV B,A
040 102	117	MOV C,A
040 103	076	MVI A,XXX
040 104	XXX	
040 105	315	CALL 000 053
040 106	053	
040 107	000	
040 110	005	DCR B
040 111	014	INR C
040 112	303	JMP 040 103
040 113	103	
040 114	040	

Page 88

REGISTER F	BINARY	SIGN BIT	ZERO BIT
0 0 3	(00000011)	0	0
1 2 6	(01010110)	0	1
2 0 6	(10000110)	1	0
1 2 7	(01010111)	0	1
0 0 2	(00000010)	0	0

Page 91

ADDRESS	OP CODE (OCTAL)	MNEMONIC	REGISTERS A (IN OCTAL)	F	S	Z	C
040 100	**227**	SUB A					
040 101	**166**	HLT (#1)*	000	126	0	1	0
040 102	**306**	ADI 001	**001**	**002**	0	0	0
040 103	**001**						
040 104	**166**	HLT (#2)	001	002	0	0	0
040 105	**306**	ADI 176					
040 106	**176**						
040 107	**166**	HLT (#3)	177	002	0	0	0
040 110	**306**	ADI 001					
040 111	**001**						
040 112	**166**	HLT (#4)	200	222	1	0	0

Answers to Questions

040 113	306	ADI 177					
040 114	177						
040 115	166	HLT (#5)	377	206	1	0	0
040 116	306	ADI 001					
040 117	001						
040 120	166	HLT (#6)	000	127	0	1	1
040 121	306	ADI 100					
040 122	100						
040 123	166	HLT (#7)	100	002	0	0	0
040 124	306	ADI 301					
040 125	301						
040 126	166	HLT (#8)	001	003	0	0	1
040 127	306	ADI 376					
040 130	376						
040 131	166	HLT (#9)	377	206	1	0	0
040 132	306	ADI 377					
040 133	377						
040 134	166	HLT (#10)	376	223	1	0	1
040 135	303	JMP 040 100					
040 136	100						
040 137	040						

Page 92

HLT #	REGISTER A F (OCTAL)		REGISTER A F (BINARY)		S	Z	C
1	000	126	00000000	01010110	0	1	0
2	001	002	00000001	00000010	0	0	0
3	177	002	01111111	00000010	0	0	0
4	200	222	10000000	10010010	1	0	0
5	377	206	11111111	10000110	1	0	0
6	000	127	00000000	01010111	0	1	1
7	100	002	01000000	00000010	0	0	0
8	001	003	00000001	00000011	0	0	1
9	377	206	11111111	10000110	1	0	0
10	376	223	11111110	10010011	1	0	1

S	Z	C	
0	0	0	See HALT #2, 3, 7
0	0	1	HALT #8
0	1	0	HALT #1
0	1	1	HALT #6
1	0	0	HALT #4, 5, 9
1	0	1	HALT #10
1	1	0	Not possible if sign bit = 1, number can't be zero
1	1	1	Not possible if sign bit = 1, number can't be zero

Page 105

The + key should give 10 beeps.
The − key should give 11 beeps.
The * key should give 12 beeps.
The / key should give 13 beeps.
The # key should give 14 beeps.
The • key should give 15 beeps.

Page 110

Guessing Game Using RND

ADDRESS	CODE	INSTRUCTION	COMMENT
040 100	303	JMP 040 200	Go get a random number.
040 101	200		
040 102	040		
040 103	103	MOV B,E	Move to B, the contents of E.
040 104	315	CALL 003 260	Call the INPUT subroutine.
040 105	260		
240 106	003		
040 107	220	SUB B	Subtract B from A.
040 110	302	JNZ 040 104	If the two numbers are not the same, jump back to 040 104Q.
040 111	104		
040 112	040		
040 113	026	MVI D,003	Move 003Q into register D. (Register D is the BEEP counter.)
040 114	003		
040 115	076	MVI A,200	Set the BEEP length.
040 116	200		
040 117	315	CALL 002 140	Call BEEP.
040 120	140		
040 121	002		
040 122	076	MVI A,200	Set the DELAY length.
040 123	200		
040 124	315	CALL 000 053	Call DELAY.
040 125	053		
040 126	000		
040 127	025	DCR D	Decrement the BEEP counter.
040 130	302	JNZ 040 115	If the BEEP counter ≠ 0 then jump back and BEEP some more.
040 131	115		
040 132	040		

Answers to Questions

040 133	303	JMP 040 100	Jump back to the beginning.
040 134	100		
040 135	040		

Guessing Game with Guess Counter

ADDRESS	CODE	INSTRUCTION	COMMENT
040 100	303	JMP 040 200	Go get a random number.
040 101	200		
040 102	040		
040 103	103	MOV B,E	Move to B, the contents of E.
040 104	016	MVI C,000	Set register C to zero. (Register C
040 105	000		will be the *guess* counter.)
040 106	315	CALL 003 260	Call the INPUT subroutine.
040 107	260		
040 110	003		
040 111	014	INR C	Increment register C (Guess + 1).
040 112	220	SUB B	Subtract B from A.
040 113	302	JNZ 040 106	If the two numbers are not the same
040 114	106		then jump back to 040 106Q.
040 115	040		
040 116	026	MVI D,003	Set the BEEP counter to 003Q.
040 117	003		
040 120	076	MVI A,200	Set the BEEP length.
040 121	200		
040 122	315	CALL 002 140	Call BEEP.
040 123	140		
040 124	002		
040 125	076	MVI A,200	Set the DELAY length.
040 126	200		
040 127	315	CALL 000 053	Call DELAY.
040 130	053		
040 131	000		
040 132	025	DCR D	Decrement the BEEP counter.
040 133	302	JNZ 040 120	If the BEEP counter ≠ 0 then jump
040 134	120		back and BEEP some more.
040 135	040		
040 136	303	JMP 040 100	Jump back to the beginning.
040 137	100		
040 140	040		

After you guess the computer's number (after the BEEPs), register C will contain the number of guesses it took.

Page 113

DECIMAL DIGIT	BINARY BYTE	OCTAL BYTE	DISPLAY LOOKS LIKE
0	10000001	201	
1	11110011	363	
2	11001000	310	
3	11100000	340	
4	10110010	262	
5	10100100	244	
6	10000100	204	
7	11110001	361	
8	10000000	200	
9	10110000	260	

Page 119

Store bytes 000Q through 100Q at addresses 040 200Q through 040 300Q:

ADDRESS	CODE	INSTRUCTION	COMMENT
040 100	041	LXI H,040 200	Load H with 040Q and L with 200Q.
040 101	200		Register pair HL now refers to
040 102	040		address 040 200Q.

Answers to Questions

040 103	076	MVI A,000	Move 000Q into the accumulator.
040 104	000		
040 105	167	MOV M,A	Move to M, the contents of A. Move the data byte in register A to address HL.
040 106	043	INX H	Increment address HL.
040 107	074	INR A	Increment the accumulator.
040 110	376	CPI 100	Compare A with 100Q.
040 111	100		
040 112	302	JNZ 040 105	If not 100Q, then jump back to address 040 105Q.
040 113	105		
040 114	040		
040 115	166	HLT	Halt.

Page 120

1. At the beginning of the program the accumulator is set to 001Q; after the program is run, the accumulator again contains 001Q — here's what happened:

LOOP #	ACCUMULATOR CONTAINS
Beginning	00000001
1	00000010
2	00000100
3	00001000
4	00010000
5	00100000
6	01000000
7	10000000
8	00000001

2. Program to count the number of *rotates*:

ADDRESS	CODE	INSTRUCTION	COMMENT
040 100	076	MVI A,001	Put 001Q into the accumulator.
040 101	001		
040 102	006	MVI B,000	Put 000Q into register B. B will be used to count the *rotates*.
040 103	000		
040 104	004	INR B	Increment the counter.
040 105	007	RLC	Rotate the accumulator left.

```
040 106    322    JNC 040 104   Jump to 040 104Q if no Carry
040 107    104                  occurred.
040 110    040

040 111    166    HLT           Stop.
```

3. Remember that 00001000 (010Q) is eight.

Page 121

After running the program, the accumulator should contain 106Q or 01000110B, which is a decimal seventy.

A different way to multiply by ten is to add a number to itself ten times—for instance, let's say the number is decimal 7. To multiply 7 times 10:

```
     7
   + 7
   + 7
   + 7
   + 7
   + 7
   + 7
   + 7
   + 7
   + 7
   ___
   = 70
```

The program to accomplish this would be simple using the ADI 007 instruction—or maybe by moving 007Q into register B, and then using the ADD B instruction.

Page 125

1. AND:

```
00100101    11110000    10101010    00001111    11000011
10001000    00001111    11111111    10101010    00000111
_____    _____    _____    _____    _____
00000000    00000000    10101010    00001010    00000011


00000000    11001010    01011111    11111111    01111111
01110101    00110101    11111111    00000000    01100010
_____    _____    _____    _____    _____
00000000    00000000    01011111    00000000    01100010
```

Answers to Questions

2. OR:

```
  00100101      11110000      10101010      00001111      11000011
  10001000      00001111      11111111      10101010      00000111
  --------      --------      --------      --------      --------
  10101101      11111111      11111111      10101111      11000111

  00000000      11001010      01011111      11111111      01111111
  01110101      00110101      11111111      00000000      01100010
  --------      --------      --------      --------      --------
  01110101      11111111      11111111      11111111      01111111
```

3. Any byte ANDed with 11111111B will result in the same byte.

4. Any byte ORed with 11111111B will result in 11111111B.

5. Any byte ANDed with 00000000B will result in 00000000B.

6. Any byte ORed with 00000000B will result in that same byte.

Page 128

With 022Q stored at 041 021Q, and 001Q stored at 041 022Q the accumulator should contain 064Q (00110100B) when the program halts.

Page 129

Change the data byte at address 041 014Q from 007Q to 017Q, and the number generated will never be larger than 00001111B.

It's easy to see how to modify the program to simulate the roll of five dice — just add three more *sections*, each section consisting of:

1. CALL RND.
2. Make sure the number is not zero.
3. Make sure the number is not seven.
4. Output the number to the proper display digit.

The only difficulty in writing the program is that *five* display digits are needed — one for each die, and that would require five output subroutines!

Appendix VII

8080 Reference Table

Returns		In		Stack		H/L		Pairs	
RET	311	IN	333	PUSH BC	305	XCHG	353	STAX B	002
RNZ	300	ddd		PUSH DE	325	XTHL	343	STAX D	022
RZ	310			PUSH HL	345	SPHL	371	LDAX B	012
RNC	320	**Out**		PUSH AF	365	PCHL	351	LDAX D	032
RC	330	OUT	323	POP BC	301			LXI B	001
RP	360	ddd		POP DE	321	**Accumulator**		nnn	
RM	370			POP HL	341	ADI	306	mmm	
		Calls		POP AF	361	ddd		LXI D	021
Jumps		CALL	315			SUI	326	nnn	
JMP	303	nnn		**Registers**		ddd		mmm	
nnn		mmm		ADD r	20X	ANI	346	LXI H	041
mmm		CNZ	304	ADC r	21X	ddd		nnn	
JNZ	302	nnn		SUB r	22X	XRI	356	mmm	
nnn		mmm		ANA r	24X	ddd		LXI SP	061
mmm		CZ	314	XRA r	25X	ORI	366	nnn	
JZ	312	nnn		ORA r	26X	ddd		mmm	
nnn		mmm		CMP r	27X	CPI	376		
mmm		CNC	324			ddd		**Incr Pair**	
JNC	322	nnn		**Increment**				INX B	003
nnn		mmm		INR r	0X4	**Direct**		INX D	023
mmm		CC	334			SHLD	042	INX H	043
JC	332	nnn		**Decrement**		nnn		INX SP	063
nnn		mmm		DCR r	0X5	mmm			
mmm		CP	364	**Moves**		LHLD	052	**Decr Pair**	
JP	362	nnn		MOV r,r	1DS	nnn		DCX B	013
nnn		mmm		MVI r	0X6	mmm		DCX D	033
mmm		CM	374	ddd		STA	062	DCX H	053
JM	372	nnn				nnn		DCX SP	073
nnn		mmm		**No-Op**		mmm			
mmm		**Shifts**		NOP	000	LDA	072		
		RLC	007			nnn			
		RRC	017	**Codes**		mmm			
		RAR	027	B = 0					
		RAL	037	C = 1					
				D = 2					
				E = 3					
				H = 4					
				L = 5					
				M = 6					
				A = 7					

Index

accumulator 1, 26
add immediate—ADI 36, 153
add register—ADD R 53, 155
address 7
addressing 7
alter key 14
AND 123, 156
AND/OR logic 123
ASCII 167

beep subroutine 77, 78
binary 2
bit 2
branch instructions 63
breakpoint 30
byte 2

call 78, 151
carry bit 89
central processor—CPU 1
conditional jumps 95

decrement register—DCR R 54, 155
decrement register pair—DCX 118, 157
delay subroutine 77, 80
Dice game 131
direct instructions 34, 59
display 1, 13

examine a program 36
exclusive-or—XOR 124, 156

flowcharts 66

halt—HLT 27
hex 161
Hi-Lo game 137

immediate instructions 35, 60
increment register—INR R 54, 155
increment register pair—INX 118, 157
input—IN 150
input subroutine 103

jump—JMP 63, 64, 150
jump if zero—JZ 101, 150

keypad 14

load a program 35
load accumulator—LDA 31, 59, 154

mem key 14
memory 1, 7
memory map 18, 19
minus key (−) 18

mnemonic op codes 27
move—MOV 45, 155
move immediate—MVI 27, 43, 155

no operation—NOP 75, 149

octal 5
op-codes 27, 191
operand 36
OR 124, 156
output—OUT 150
output subroutine 111, 140

PAM-8 13
plus key (+) 18
POP 50, 157
processor status word—PSW 85
programming 27
PUSH 50, 157

random access memory—RAM 18
random numbers 109, 127, 165
read only memory—ROM 18
register 1, 26, 43
register instructions 60
register pairs 117
register roll 46, 47
rotate accumulator 119, 153
run a program

sign bit 86
split octal 5, 8, 9
stack 49, 157
Stars game 141
status bits 85
stop a program 36
store accumulator—STA 27, 59, 154
subtract immediate—SUI 70, 153
subtract register—SUB R 53, 156

terminal 1
tracing 30

zero bit 86